Preface

During my career as a pharmacy educator and employer, I have analyzed hundreds of résumés and curricula vitae and have conducted even more interviews. I've noticed that many people who are seeking pharmacy positions, although they are competent and knowledgeable, do not devote the attention they should to their written communications and interviewing skills. This oversight detracts from the positive impression they would otherwise make. My mission in this book is to help people in all facets of the profession, from technicians and new graduates to veteran pharmacists, land interviews and carry them off with aplomb.

The Pharmacy Professional's Guide to Résumés, CVs, & Interviewing is about creating a favorable image with employers, admissions committees, and selection panels. It offers insights for preparing powerful résumés, curricula vitae, and cover letters, coaches you about coming across professionally in interviews, and helps you formulate effective answers to frequently asked interview questions. Although many publications offer similar guidance, this book's unique focus is pharmacy professionals—those entering the profession, seeking an initial position, changing positions, choosing new directions, or returning to the profession after a hiatus.

Pulling together straightforward advice for pharmacists about the "perfect" résumé, CV, letter, or interview question is challenging because each segment of the profession has its own opinions and biases. Consequently, this book—the result of my own experience as well as countless conversations with employers and applicants—should be seen as a resource to help you shape the approach that is right for you. It is not definitive and the sample documents included should not be viewed as templates.

Be sure to seek input from colleagues, peers, and mentors throughout the process. Their assistance, together with the wisdom in this book, should put you well on your way to obtaining your ideal pharmacy career position.

Thomas P. Reinders

Chapter 1

Assessing Your Career Goals

Contrary to what you may think, developing your résumé is not the first step in searching for a job. Before you even put pen to paper, you need to carefully assess your goals, strengths, values, and preferences to gain a clear perspective on where you stand now and want to go in the future. Unfortunately, many people put more thought into planning their next vacation than mapping out their career. Whether you are a pharmacy technician seeking to become a pharmacist, a recent graduate seeking an entry-level position, or a seasoned pharmacist looking for a new challenge, it pays to think through your goals—and then prepare a résumé designed to realize them.

The Career Pathway Evaluation Program

You may believe it's easy to select a career option in the pharmacy profession. But if you do a little research, you will find that the career possibilities go far beyond the traditional areas of community pharmacy or hospital practice. Table 1.1, taken from the American Pharmacists Association's Career Pathway Evaluation Program for Pharmacy Professionals, lists the many directions pharmacy professionals can follow.

The Career Pathway Evaluation Program identifies 25 career options ranging from academia to regulatory affairs.[1] Pharmacy schools use this program to help students make informed career decisions. Individual pharmacists investigating new options find it helpful, too. You can access the program, which includes exercises and a workbook, from the American Pharmacists Association's Web site at www.aphanet.org/pathways/pathways.html

TO ACCESS THE APhA CAREER PATHWAY EVALUATION PROGRAM, DESIGNED TO HELP YOU IDENTIFY THE PHARMACY CAREER OPTION APPROPRIATE FOR YOU, GO TO WWW.APHANET.ORG/PATHWAYS/PATHWAYS.HTML

Critical Job Factors

For each career option, the Career Pathway Evaluation Program details 34 critical job factors that you can use to evaluate which paths best suit you. The box on page 5 lists these critical factors. They represent six distinct areas including: (1) future innovation and job fulfillment, (2) translating knowledge to pharmacy practice, (3) relational, (4) workload, (5) non-salary compensation, and (6) freedom.

Reviewing these factors will give you an idea of how much patient counseling, professional interaction, problem solving, multitasking, thinking innovatively, applying scientific or medical knowledge, and managing a business is involved in each career path. The summaries also cover such matters as work schedule, the amount of pressure involved, job security, prestige, income, and opportunities for advancement.

You should think about all these things carefully as you look at potential career choices.

Many excellent books, workshops, and career counseling centers can also help you. Start by calling your local community college or a nearby university to find out about career development workshops.

Self-Assessment Survey Tool

The Career Pathway Evaluation Program has a convenient self-assessment survey tool that takes just 20 to 30 minutes. Upon completion, you will receive a set of scores with your possible career matches based on an assessment of all 34 critical factors. A second set of scores will outline which critical factors you consider most important. Each score links to a specific pharmacy career profile that contains a background description of the position, an insider's perspective about what aspects of the position they find most and least appealing, and a brief commentary about how pharmacists in this career option rated each of the individual critical factors.

The program offers additional insight about career planning through a series of interactive

Table 1.1
Career Options for Pharmacy Professionals

COMMUNITY

Chain
Apothecary
Clinical*
Consultation
Franchise
Home Health Care
Long Term Care
Medical Group Affiliate

Managed Care
Clinical*

Independent
Clinical*
Compounding Specialist
Consultation
Franchise
Home Health Care
Long Term Care
Medical Group Affiliate
Office Based Practice

INSTITUTION

Hospital (University, Community, Government)
Administration
Ambulatory Care
Clinical*
Distribution and Control
Nuclear

Long Term Care

Veterinary

CONSULTING
Clinical*
Consumer
Home Health Care
JCAHO
Long Term Care
Managed Care
Management/Resource Evaluation
Medicare/Medicaid

REGULATORY

State
Board of Pharmacy
Consumer Affairs
Department of Health
Legislature

Medicare/Medicaid

Federal
Alcohol and Drug Abuse
Congress
Mental Health

Armed Services
Drug Enforcement Agency
Department of Health & Human Services
Food & Drug Administration
Health Care Financing Administration
Indian/Public Health Service
Veterans Administration

INDUSTRY

Administration
Professional Relations

Business
Management
Marketing
Sales

Research and Development
Administration
Basic Research
Biological Sciences
Clinical Research
Medicinal Chemistry
Pharmaceuticals
Pharmacognosy

Technical/Scientific
Drug Information
Manufacturing
Post Marketing Surveillance
Product Quality Control
Regulatory Affairs

ACADEMIA
Administration
Biological Sciences
Clinical*
Continuing Education
Experiential Education
Medicinal Chemistry
Pharmaceutics
Pharmacognosy
Pharmacology

Pharmacotherapy
Pharmacy Administration
Pharmacy Practice
Pharmacoeconomics

OTHER
Association Management
Automation Technology
Computer Technology
Contract Research Organization
Mail Service
Public Policy and Law
Publishing and Communications
Third Party Insurance
United States Pharmacopeia
Wholesaler

* Clinical areas of focus include:
Ambulatory Care
Cardiology
Critical Care
Dermatology
Drug Information
Emergency Medicine
Endocrinology
Gastroenterology
Geriatrics
Hematology
Immunology
Infectious Diseases
Internal Medicine
Intravenous Therapy
Neurology
Nutrition
Oncology
Pain Management
Pediatrics
Pharmacokinetics
Poison Control
Psychiatry
Rheumatology
Substance Abuse
Surgery
Toxicology
Transplantation

Adapted from APhA Career Pathway Evaluation Program for Pharmacy Professionals, American Pharmacists Association.

group exercises. Even without the benefit of a group, you can complete the exercises on your own to enhance your planning process. Some of the components include an assessment of what you know about career choices, your decision making style, and the assignment of weights and values to each of the critical factors. The latter process allows you to complete a decision matrix that provides a reasonable basis for comparing career options.

You will benefit from the time you take to complete the survey and explore the exercises. For prospective students or pharmacy technicians, the program will provide you with a thorough overview of career options as well as information about whether your personal strengths match those outlined for pharmacists in a variety of practice settings. For pharmacy students and new graduates, the program offers an opportunity to assess which career options best suit your personal interests and strengths. Also, it will help detect areas that need strengthening with post-graduate study or training experiences. For practicing pharmacists, the program offers the ability to prioritize your professional needs and relate them to practice areas which will most likely satisfy these needs. This may require a change in practice settings or even additional education and training.

Thinking Globally

Despite the practice setting, the health care employee marketplace has changed so markedly in the past decade that pharmacists must meet entirely new expectations. In her book *Career Intelligence*, Barbara Moses lists 12 rules to follow to achieve career success in today's world. The box on the following page outlines these rules. Successful workers in the "new economy"—an environment characterized by technology, information, and reengineering—think globally, remain sensitive to diverse cultures, and have powerful communication skills.

TWELVE RULES FOR CAREER SUCCESS

1. Ensure your marketability by building effective networks of colleagues.

2. Think globally. Today, geographic borders have disappeared and the entire world represents a potential market. Your ability to interact with other cultures comfortably will give you a distinct advantage.

3. Develop effective communication skills so you can get your message across in powerful and persuasive ways. This includes conventional communication approaches, such as graphics and the Internet.

4. Commit yourself to life-long learning. Employers like applicants who take personal responsibility for learning, both within and outside the work environment.

5. Understand business trends facing the profession, including economic, demographic, and cultural factors.

6. Prepare for areas of competence rather than merely focusing on routine tasks and duties. You must develop skill sets and knowledge systems that you can transfer to a variety of different settings.

7. Seek to understand the profession's future by monitoring demographic, economic, and cultural trends.

8. Manage career effectiveness by building financial independence and soundly handling personal finances.

9. Discard the traditional notion of "career ladders" and envision a lattice instead, since you may need to move laterally to achieve upward mobility.

10. When deciding whether to pursue specialization or follow the path of a generalist, conduct an objective assessment of personal goals. For example, do you want to focus on technical aspects of the profession? Are you interested in clinical research? Do you hope to expand your credentials?

11. Learn to manage your time effectively and know your priorities and limitations.

12. Take note of your successes and avoid dwelling on your mistakes or shortcomings. Instead document your achievements so that you have a record of the many things you do well.

Adapted from: Moses B. *Career Intelligence.* San Francisco: Berrett-Koehler Publishers, Inc; 1998.

SAMPLE OBJECTIVES

- A pharmacy internship position that will enhance my education and practice experience.

- A tenure-eligible faculty position in pharmaceutics.

- To join a health-system pharmacy where I can apply my knowledge and expertise as a drug information specialist.

Developing a Career Objective

Identifying a specific area of interest within the pharmacy profession will help you communicate to others exactly what you want and enhance your chances for success. You can state this area of interest at the beginning of a résumé or curriculum vitae (CV) in the form of a "career objective." Because a career objective is a long-range plan, consider using the term "objective" by itself when your wording in this section is linked specifically to the position you wish to fill.

Pinpointing Your Objective

To pinpoint your objective, systematically assess your strengths, abilities, knowledge, skills, interests, and values. You also need to evaluate career options to identify possible matches for you. A few possible career alternatives you might include in your objective are:

- To obtain a pharmacy technician position.

- To obtain a pharmacy intern position.

- To obtain a pharmacy practice residency position.

- To obtain a pharmacy fellowship position.

- To obtain a pharmacist position.

- To obtain a pharmacy management position.

- To obtain a clinical pharmacist position.

- To obtain a faculty position.

Be Clear, Succinct

After narrowing your choices to the objective that suits you best, you must communicate it clearly and succinctly. Including your objective in your résumé or CV is considered optional, but expressing it with clarity—even if only for yourself—will help you identify the results you're seeking from your job search. The box on page 3 includes sample career objectives for someone seeking a pharmacy-related position.

Personal Statements

In some instances you may need to expand your career objective into a "personal statement." You are most likely to be asked for a personal statement if you apply to a pharmacy school, a residency program, a fellowship program, or a graduate program. To get you started, you may be supplied an open-ended question such as, "What led you to choose a career in pharmacy?" or "How will this program help you reach your professional goals?" Stay within whatever word limit you are given, and if none is supplied, aim for about 500 words.

Practicing pharmacists can also incorporate a personal statement into a letter of introduction to a prospective employer or include it as an element of an electronic portfolio. Details on how to prepare a personal statement are beyond the scope of this book, but the general pointers below should help you get started. Working through the APhA Career Pathway Evaluation Program is also likely to spark ideas for preparing a powerful personal statement.

- Do not rush the process. Take time to prepare a personal statement that is focused and well thought out.

- Do your best to be original so you stand out from the crowd. At the same time, you must come across as sincere—do not pretend to be the "ideal candidate."

- Reveal something about yourself so the reader relates to you and wants to get to know you better.

- Reflect on how your education and employment experiences have contributed to your personal and professional growth.

- Discuss specific strengths such as leadership or communication skills and why they are an advantage in the position you seek.

- Give examples or anecdotes that back up your points. A brief story that shows your positive attributes is more powerful than merely telling about them.

- Consider identifying hardships you have overcome and how the experience has strengthened your personal characteristics such as motivation, empathy, or persistence.

- Address features of the position or program that are unique and most appealing to you.

- Keep the statement's tone positive.

- Avoid recounting information in your résumé, curriculum vitae, or portfolio.

Planning a Career Transition

With all the different career options available, many pharmacists consider change. For various reasons ranging from termination to entering the workforce after raising a family, you need to honestly appraise your personal and professional assets before starting to search for a new position. In some cases, you may need to obtain additional education (e.g., a nontraditional Doctor of Pharmacy degree or graduate degree) or skills (e.g., certification in a specialty area) to realistically obtain your ideal position.

Developing a Search Strategy

When searching for a position, first you need to identify potential employers. Many strategies exist, such as using the services of professional recruiters, reviewing advertisements in newspapers or professional journals, or looking at electronic listings of positions on the World Wide Web—but these do not always prove successful. In the pharmacy community, networking brings the most fruitful results for pinpointing key opportunities. In fact, most health professionals say that the best way to find positions suited to your needs and talents is to avail yourself of personal contacts: peers, coworkers, and people you know at pharmacy schools, corporations, health systems, and professional organizations.

Have your résumé, CV, or portfolio ready to go before you learn of a promising opportunity. Also submit a well-crafted cover letter that expresses your interest in the position and requests an interview. The chapters that follow detail effective ways to prepare your résumé, CV, and portfolio, get ready for interviews, and manage other aspects of the job search.

Keep in mind that your career goals will probably change over time. You will continually update your résumé, CV, or portfolio to reflect your current situation throughout your life. No matter what stage of life you've reached, it's worthwhile to step back and ask yourself, Am I achieving what I want? Does my job contribute to, or detract from, my happiness? Am I comfortable with my career path, or do I want to change career directions? Do I need to develop new skills? Am I doing all I can to maintain and strengthen my knowledge? If the answers you come up with lead you to seek new opportunities, having a current résumé, CV, or portfolio brings a big advantage.

Reference

1. APhA Career Pathway Evaluation Program for Pharmacy Professionals. Washington D.C.: American Pharmacists Association; 2005.

CRITICAL JOB FACTORS

The Career Pathway Evaluation Program for Pharmacy Professionals lists the following critical factors you can use to evaluate which career choices are best for you.

- Interaction with public
- Conducting physical assessment and/or interpreting laboratory values
- Continuity of relationships
- Helping people
- Collaboration with other professionals
- Educating other professionals
- Variety of daily activities
- Multiple task handling
- Problem solving
- Focus of expertise
- Innovative thinking
- Applying scientific/medical knowledge
- Creating new knowledge by conducting research
- Management/supervisory
- Pressure/stress
- Work schedule
- Part-time opportunities
- Leisure/family time
- Job security
- Opportunities for advancement
- Opportunities for leadership development
- Community prestige
- Professional involvement
- Income
- Benefits (vacation, health, retirement)
- Geographic location
- Autonomy
- Self-worth
- Future focus
- Professional prestige
- Unique practice environment
- Advanced degree
- Entrepreneurial opportunity
- Additional training

Chapter 2

Preparing Your Résumé

Think of a résumé as a marketing tool that helps you land a job interview. A good résumé makes all the difference between getting read and being thrown away. Employers are busy. When confronted with a stack of 100 résumés, they will zip through to find those that seem to represent positive professionals who have solid skills and can get things done.

In addition to documenting your education, experience, and accomplishments, a good résumé focuses on your positive attributes and how they potentially satisfy an employer's or program's needs. Over the past decade, the approach in résumés has become increasingly "achievement oriented" to highlight job applicants' successes. Employers want to hire people who get results. By drawing attention to your unique talents and accomplishments instead of merely listing job descriptions, résumés can show the value you have brought to your work and your professional activities. Put simply, résumés should be about the *worker*, not the *work*.

You should keep your résumé brief—usually one or two typewritten pages—and set it up so that potential employers can easily pick out key facts.

Although your résumé should reflect your individuality, most follow three basic formats, outlined in the box to the left.

Résumé Basics

Résumés contain many standard and optional sections you can use, depending on your level of experience, areas of expertise, and the type of job you seek. The box on the next page highlights these elements.

Contact Information

You should always begin your résumé with your contact information, including name, address, telephone number, and e-mail address. Use either your full legal name or your first name, middle initial, and last name. Do not put the term "résumé" at the top. Instead, use your name as the title.

THREE COMMON RÉSUMÉ FORMATS

1. **CHRONOLOGICAL RÉSUMÉ:** This résumé format presents education and experience in reverse chronological order, with the most recent experience appearing first. The chronological résumé usually gets organized by job titles and emphasizes positions held and the organizations where you've worked. The résumé of Page A. Shaw in Chapter 3 (page 21) provides an example of a chronological résumé.

2. **FUNCTIONAL OR SKILLS RÉSUMÉ:** This type of résumé gets organized by the skills you have acquired through education and experience. The résumé focuses on what you want to do—the skills you hope to use in your new job—rather than what you have accomplished in the past. Functional résumés provide a good alternative when employment gaps exist or you've held many positions in a short time. The résumé of Gina Maria Ruiz in Chapter 3 (page 34) provides an example of a functional résumé.

3. **COMBINATION RÉSUMÉ:** This résumé style incorporates the best of both the functional and chronological formats. It includes both a description of positions you've held and a summary of skills you've acquired. The résumé of Amanda Ashley Sanderson in Chapter 3 (page 26) provides an example of a combination résumé.

Although all three résumé formats are acceptable, it's a safe bet to select the style that most people within your profession use. In the pharmacy community, the chronological résumé gets used most often.

Table 2.1
Action Verbs

A		
Accepted	Collated	Encouraged
Accomplished	Collected	Enforced
Achieved	Communicated	Engineered
Acknowledged	Compared	Enhanced
Acquired	Compiled	Enlisted
Adapted	Completed	Enrolled
Addressed	Compounded	Entered
Adjusted	Computed	Ensured
Administered	Computerized	Established
Advanced	Conceptualized	Estimated
Advised	Conducted	Evaluated
Aided	Conferred	Examined
Allocated	Consolidated	Exceeded
Analyzed	Constructed	Executed
Answered	Consulted	Exercised
Applied	Contacted	Exhibited
Appointed	Contracted	Expanded
Appraised	Contributed	Expedited
Apprised	Controlled	Experimented
Appropriated	Converted	Explained
Approved	Cooperated	Extended
Arbitrated	Coordinated	Extracted
Arranged	Corrected	**F**
Assembled	Corresponded	Facilitated
Assessed	Counseled	Familiarized
Assigned	Created	Filed
Assisted	Critiqued	Finalized
Assured	Customized	Focused
Attained	Cut	Followed
Attended	**D**	Forecasted
Audited	Debated	Formalized
Authored	Decided	Formed
Authorized	Decreased	Formulated
Automated	Defined	Funded
Awarded	Delegated	Furnished
B	Delivered	**G**
Balanced	Demonstrated	Gained
Briefed	Described	Generated
Budgeted	Designed	Greeted
Built	Detected	Guided
C	Determined	**H**
Calculated	Developed	
Calibrated	Devised	Handled
Captured	Directed	Headed
Cared for	Discovered	Hired
Catalogued	Dispensed	Hosted
Centralized	Displayed	**I**
Certified	Distributed	Identified
Chaired	Documented	Illustrated
Charted	Drafted	Implemented
Changed	**E**	Improved
Checked	Edited	Incorporated
Chose	Educated	Increased
Classified	Eliminated	Indexed
Coached	Employed	Individualized
Collaborated	Enabled	Influenced
	Enacted	Informed

People with two addresses—which is especially common among students—should list both addresses and related contact information to minimize the chance of communication gaps. You don't want to compromise your chances of landing an interview or a position simply because the employer couldn't reach you.

Career Objective

Including a career objective on your résumé is considered optional by recruitment experts. Many pharmacists and health professionals omit career statements from their résumés. If you choose to include one, be sure your objective is clearly stated. Some people fear that including a career objective on their résumé will give too narrow a view of their interests. When written properly, however, a career statement can highlight how your experience and skills relate to the position you desire.

Basically, a career objective provides a brief, clear statement detailing the type of position you want and how your skills qualify you for the job. Directly echoing the needs of an employer or program director will increase the likelihood that they will consider your résumé for further review. Chapter 1 includes several examples of career objectives.

When writing your statement, avoid generic phrases such as "seeking a position with opportunity for advancement" or "seeking a challenging position for professional growth." Most importantly, make sure your career statement closely matches the position you seek.

Summary Statement

In addition to a career objective, you can also include a summary statement on your résumé. A summary statement highlights your unique abilities or experiences that a reviewer might not easily detect in a quick review of your résumé. Place your summary statement directly after your career objective.

PRIMARY ELEMENTS OF A RÉSUMÉ

- Contact information
- Summary statement (optional)
- Career objective (optional)
- Education
- Experience
- Memberships and service
- Awards and honors

OTHER POSSIBILITIES

- Licenses and certificates
- Committees
- Personal interests or activities
- Research interests
- Publications, editorships, presentations
- Special skills
- Special training and continuing education
- Leadership positions
- References

Opinions vary on the value of summary statements. Although many health professionals do not include them, use of these statements is growing in most other sectors. A well-written, effective summary is a snapshot of your background, quickly focusing readers on the essence of your résumé and compelling them to continue on to the details. Some people in hiring positions say they like the way summary statements quickly call attention to key strengths. If you use a summary statement, however, the material in the rest of your résumé must back up its assertions. For example, if you claim to have leadership skills, the experience and accomplishments cited in the body of your résumé must show that you have taken initiative, headed groups, and motivated others.

Education

Educational experience provides employers with critical information. List the name and location of the institution, dates attended, and the type of degree you earned in reverse chronological order. If you are still pursuing a degree, list the date that you expect you will earn the degree (for example, "degree expected May 2007"). You can use the term "degree in progress" if you do not know your expected date of graduation.

If you took only one or two courses at a college or university to fulfill a degree requirement, you usually do not need to list that institution. Likewise, do not include high school credentials unless you have attended college for less than two years.

If you include high school information in your educational experience, put it just after the college information (reverse chronological order) and state the school's name and location, dates attended, and diploma earned.

Pre-pharmacy students and technician candidates without a college degree who have completed college courses relevant to an available position (chemistry or biology courses, for example) can consider listing them under a heading such as "relevant course work."

ACADEMIC STANDING

Recent graduates often include information about their academic standing in the education section of their résumé. Some list a cumulative grade point average or class standing, especially if they have been an "A" or "B" student. Others rely on a statement about their graduation honor to convey their academic success (e.g., graduated cum laude). Although an excellent approach, keep in mind that the ways different colleges and universities define grade points for graduation honors may vary. For example, out of a possible 4.0 cumulative grade point average, cum laude may range from between 3.30 to 3.59; magna cum laude from 3.5 to 3.89; and summa cum laude from 3.8 to 4.0.

Table 2.1, *continued*
Action Verbs

Initiated	Originated	Revitalized
Innovated	Outlined	Routed
Inspected	Outsourced	
Installed		**S**
Instituted	**P**	Saved
Instructed	Packaged	Scanned
Integrated	Participated	Scheduled
Interacted	Patented	Screened
Interfaced	Performed	Searched
Interpreted	Persuaded	Secured
Interviewed	Planned	Selected
Introduced	Prepared	Served
Invented	Presented	Shaped
Inventoried	Presided	Simplified
Investigated	Prevented	Solved
Issued	Printed	Sorted
Itemized	Prioritized	Sought
J	Processed	Specified
Joined	Procured	Sponsored
Judged	Produced	Staffed
Justified	Programmed	Standardized
L	Projected	Stimulated
Launched	Promoted	Streamlined
Lectured	Proposed	Strengthened
Led	Provided	Structured
Lessened	Publicized	Studied
Located	Published	Submitted
M	Purchased	Summarized
Maintained	**Q**	Supervised
Managed	Qualified	Supplied
Manufactured	Quantified	Supported
Marketed	**R**	Surveyed
Mastered	Received	**T**
Measured	Recognized	Tabulated
Mediated	Recommended	Taught
Mentored	Reconciled	Tested
Merged	Recorded	Traced
Met	Recruited	Trained
Modeled	Redesigned	Transcribed
Moderated	Reduced	Transferred
Modernized	Reengineered	Translated
Modified	Referred	Transmitted
Monitored	Registered	Trimmed
Motivated	Regulated	Tutored
N	Released	Typed
Negotiated	Reorganized	**U**
Nominated	Replied	Undertook
Notified	Reported	Updated
O	Represented	Upgraded
Observed	Requested	**V**
Obtained	Researched	Validated
Operated	Resolved	Verified
Optimized	Responded	Volunteered
Ordered	Restructured	**W**
Organized	Retrieved	Worked
Oriented	Reversed	Wrote
	Reviewed	
	Revised	

Common headings for the education section include "education and professional training" or "academic degrees and postgraduate training." Here you can include such programs as residencies, fellowships, or technician training programs. You should list such programs in reverse chronological order and supply the name and location of the institution, dates attended, and the type of certificate or credential earned. Provide the name of the program director or major preceptor, as well as the accreditation status of the program, if desired.

Some people like to include their professional training as a separate section, especially if they've completed a residency or specialized program that they want to highlight. This usually depends on your personal preference. Sometimes the final decision comes down to how much space you have on the page.

Experience

Employers focus sharply on the experience section of the résumé. In the early stages of your career you may find this section challenging to prepare, since your professional experiences may include work outside the profession. As your career develops and you acquire more experience, you can fill this section with professional work.

Information about your experience should include the name and location of the agency or institution, beginning and ending dates of service, title of the position held, and a description of key duties that uses active, energetic phrasing and cites accomplishments. Be selective—highlight responsibilities that demonstrate initiative and special skills as opposed to listing each item on your job description.

Organizational Considerations

How you organize the experience section of your résumé depends on the type of résumé you prepare.

Chronological Résumés

In the chronological résumé—commonly used by pharmacy professionals—you start with your most recent position. Listing each position in reverse chronological order helps accentuate a consistent pattern of employment. When using this format, however, you may need to leave part-time or short-term positions out. If you're concerned about a potential employer's reaction to "employment gaps," go ahead and list your part-time or short-term employment.

Functional Résumés

In functional résumés, you organize the experience section according to skills that relate to the position sought. When using this format, make sure you also include employers, position titles, and years of experience.

Combination Résumés

A combination of the chronological and functional résumés allows for creativity and individuality. For example, you can list employers in a chronological fashion while including the various skills acquired with each employer.

Volunteer Experience

In the experience section of your résumé you can also include volunteer experience, especially if you have sustained your commitment for a year or more and you've demonstrated an ability to apply your knowledge and skills. The experience gained through volunteerism, especially in an activity related to health care, can provide as much value as experience acquired through a paid position.

Achievements

Regardless of format, make your résumé achievement oriented. Lace it generously with achievements rather than giving a bland list of job duties and activities.

When detailing positions and related accomplishments, make your statements clear, concise, and action oriented. Organize your material in short bullet statements. Use the present tense to describe your current job, and past tense for the others.

RÉSUMÉ DON'TS

When developing your résumé, do not include:

- Your Social Security number
- Your age
- Your gender
- Your marital status or spouse's name
- Your health status or disabilities
- Your children's names and ages
- Your height and weight
- Your race, ethnic background, or religion

Action Verbs

When describing your experiences and accomplishments, use action verbs and avoid excess wordiness. For example, instead of "vaccines were administered," say "administered vaccines." Rather than "had responsibility for counseling patients," say "counseled patients."

Action verbs are your ally as you underscore your achievements. You should never stretch the truth, but by all means state your activities in the best possible light. "Created" sounds much more impressive than "began," for example. Words such as "worked on" or "handled" can be replaced with "produced," "developed," or "prepared." Table 2.1 lists commonly used action verbs in pharmacy-related résumés.

Special Skills

Highlighting special skills you have—such as experience with specific computer software or laboratory equipment—may give you a unique advantage when competing for a position. Some people create a heading in the résumé entitled "special skills" to accentuate this information. You can also include a heading such as "licenses and certificates" for professional licenses (pharmacist, pharmacy intern) and certificates (pharmacy technician, cardiopulmonary resuscitation training, Board of Pharmaceutical Specialties certification) if you have not included this information elsewhere in your résumé.

Memberships and Service

Include memberships and service roles in your résumé, especially those related to professional activities. In addition to years of membership, list any offices held or specific recognition gained, which demonstrates your potential leadership ability. This section is also a good place to document community service activities.

Awards and Honors

List any awards, honors, or other recognition you've received. If you've earned a lot of accolades, you may want to create a special section for them. Otherwise, list them

Table 2.2
Questions for References

How long have you known the person and in what capacity?

How well do you know the applicant?

What is your estimate of the applicant's academic ability?

Can the applicant apply his or her knowledge and skills?

How would you describe the quality of the applicant's work?

How would you rate the applicant's written communication skills?

How would you rate the applicant's verbal communication skills?

Do you find the applicant dependable and reliable?

Does the applicant complete assignments on time?

Does the applicant exercise good judgment?

Does the applicant accept constructive criticism?

How would you assess the applicant's creativity and ability to solve problems?

Does the applicant display enthusiasm?

Does the applicant demonstrate the ability to organize and manage time in an efficient manner?

Is the applicant a leader?

How would you describe the applicant's emotional stability and level of maturity?

How would you rate the applicant's motivation?

How would you rate the applicant's initiative?

How would you rate the applicant's assertiveness?

What is your impression of the applicant's integrity?

Does the applicant demonstrate the ability to work effectively with peers?

Is the applicant committed to professional practice?

What is the applicant's reputation as a pharmacy practitioner?

What is the applicant's reputation as a researcher?

Does the applicant exhibit effective administrative and management skills?

What is the applicant's reputation as a teacher?

What do you consider the applicant's strengths?

What do you consider the applicant's weaknesses?

What is your overall assessment of the applicant?

Do you know of anything that would disqualify the applicant from further consideration?

Can you think of anything I should know about the applicant that I have not asked?

somewhere else in your résumé. For example, you could include a service award in the "activities" section of your résumé.

The honors and awards section can include major grants, publications, or invited presentations. Although such information usually appears in the curriculum vitae, it may help to highlight a significant grant award or published research article in your résumé.

References

References should not appear on the résumé unless the prospective employer specifically requests it. They take up valuable space and may differ depending on the position you seek. Some résumés say "references available upon request" at the bottom, but this statement is optional.

Prepare a separate sheet with references for potential employers. The reference sheet should fill no more than a single page and include the person's name, affiliation, mailing address, and telephone number. If you have a fax number and e-mail address, include them as well. You can also include a brief statement about what each reference can contribute concerning your knowledge, skills, and abilities. Before listing your references, check with each person for permission.

When potential employers contact references, they may ask questions orally or request a written assessment of your abilities. Table 2.2 lists common questions that potential employers may ask your references.

Military Service and Other Sections

Since résumés highlight your knowledge, skills, and abilities, you may need to create unique sections to accommodate your background. For example, if you served in the military you should include information about the branch of service, provide entry and discharge dates, and prepare a chronological listing that highlights your rank, type of discharge, and reserves activity.

Order of Sections

The order of your résumé sections will vary on an individual basis. Typically, pharmacy professionals start with general information and proceed to education, experience, activities, honors, and references. Optional sections include career objective, statement of qualifications, relevant course work, and special skills.

Formatting and Readability

A successful résumé should appeal to the reader's eye. It should be neat, well organized, and easily readable with clear, consistent headers. For good readability, use:

- White, off-white, or light ivory paper with a bond weight of 20 or 24 pounds.

- A font size of 10 to 14 points.

- A consistent typeface.

- Consistent line spacing.

- One-inch margins at the top, sides, and bottom.

- Section headings and breaks between sections.

- A consistent format, so that the typed copy and white space look symmetrical.

- A quality printer with black ink.

SAMPLE FONT TYPES

Serif

- **Bookman Old Style**
  asdfjklm ASDFJKLM 123

- Courier
  asdfjklm ASDFJKLM 123

- Georgia
  asdfjklm ASDFJKLM 123

- Times New Roman
  asdfjklm ASDFJKLM 123

Sans Serif

- Arial
  asdfjklm ASDFJKLM 123

- Lucida Sans
  asdfjklm ASDFJKLM 123

- Tahoma
  asdfjklm ASDFJKLM 123

- Verdana
  asdfjklm ASDFJKLM 123

Table 2.3
Keywords for Electronic Formats

A

Accreditation
Administration
Administrative support
Adverse drug reaction
Advertising
Alternative medicine
Alumni relations
Ambulatory care
Aseptic technique
Audits

B

Benchmarking
Biologicals
Biotechnology
Budget administration
Budget allocation

C

Career development
Case management
Certification
Change management
Clinical decision making
Clinical research
Clinical services
Clinical services
　　management
Clinical studies
Communication
Community outreach
Community practice
Compensation
Competitive bidding
Compounding
Computer systems
Computers
Continuity of care
Continuous quality
　　improvement
Contract administration
Contract negotiations
Controlled substances
Corporate sponsorship
Correspondence
Cost avoidance
Cost reduction
Credentialing
Curriculum development
Customer relations
Customer satisfaction
Customer service

D

Data collection
Disease management
　　program

Dispensing devices
Distribution
Documentation
Drug administration
Drug distribution
Drug distribution
　　automation
Drug distribution system
Drug evaluation
Drug information
Drug interactions
Drug metabolism
Drug therapy monitoring
Drug usage evaluation
Drug use control
Drug utilization

E

Economics
Educational
　　programming
Equipment
Errors
Ethics

F

Financial management
Formulary
Formulation
Full-time equivalent
Fundraising

G

Geriatrics
Good manufacturing
　　practices
Government affairs
Grant administration
Guidelines

H

Health maintenance
　　organization
Health care system
Health promotion
Home health care
Hospice care
Hospital

I

Immunization
Immunology
Improving health
　　outcomes
Incompatibilities
Industry
Industry relations
Infectious diseases
Information systems

Injections
Inpatient care
Instructional media
Internal medicine
Interventions
Intravenous therapy
Inventory control
Investigational drug

J

JCAHO
Just-in-time inventory

L

Labeling
Leadership development
Leadership training
Legislation
Long-term care

M

Mail order services
Managed care
Manufacturing
Marketing
Market research
Materials management
Media relations
Medication errors
Medication use
　　evaluation
Meeting planning

N

Needs assessment
Not-for-profit
Nuclear pharmacy
Nursing home
Nutrition
Nutrition support

O

Office management
Office services
Oncology
Operating budget
Order processing
Outcomes
Outcomes research
Outsourcing
Over-the-counter drugs

P

Packaging
Pain management
Patient care
Patient counseling
Patient information
Patient relations

Pediatrics
Peer review
Performance appraisal
Personnel
Pharmaceutical care
Pharmaceutical
　　technology
Pharmaceutics
Pharmacodynamics
Pharmacoeconomics
Pharmacoepidemiology
Pharmacogenetics
Pharmacogenomics
Pharmacognosy
Pharmacokinetics
Pharmacology
Pharmacopeial standards
Pharmacotherapy
Pharmacy benefit
　　management
Pharmacy practice
Poison control
Policy and procedures
Policy development
Political affairs
Practice management
Prescribing
Prescription benefit
　　management
Prescriptions
Pricing
Primary care
Procurement
Product development
Product selection
Productivity
Productivity
　　improvement
Professional competence
Professional recruitment
Project management
Project planning
Protocols
Psychiatric pharmacy
Public affairs
Public health
Public policy
　　development
Purchasing

Q

Quality assurance
Quality control
Quality improvement
Quality of care
Quality of life

R

Records management
Recruitment and
　　retention
Reengineering
Research and
　　development
Reimbursement
Request for proposal
Research
Resource management
Regulatory affairs
Retail sales
Risk management

S

Scheduling
Service delivery
Specialty
Speaker's bureau
Staffing
Standards
Strategic planning
Sterile products
Substance abuse

T

Team building
Team leadership
Technical support
Therapeutic efficacy
Therapeutic equivalency
Therapeutic substitution
Third-party payer

U

Unit dose
Utilization review

V

Vaccines
Vendor relations
Volunteer recruitment
Volunteer training

W

Wellness program
Workload

Length

Recruiters and busy personnel assistants tend to favor one-page résumés. If you don't have a lot of professional experience, you'll probably find one page enough. But if you have significant background in pharmacy, you may need to add a second page. Anyone with more than a two-page résumé should consider preparing a curriculum vitae, which is detailed in Chapter 4.

Paper

The type of paper you use can make a difference, so opt for better quality paper when possible. Look for business stationery with a bond weight of 20 or 24 pounds and more cotton fiber than regular photocopy paper. Many office suppliers carry paper products specifically labeled as "letterhead and résumé paper" that you can use with laser or ink jet printers.

Electronic Formats

In today's high-tech world where a lot of information gets sent over the Internet, you will need versions of your résumé suitable for scanning and electronic transmission. Some employers or program directors may want to scan your résumé so they can store it in an electronic database—a growing trend as technology advances. More and more, potential employers send applicants' résumés electronically to members of the search committee for their review, rather than mailing out paper photocopies. This means you need to modify your résumé to minimize the loss of content. Fancy bells and whistles do not translate well in documents that are transmitted electronically.

Preparing a Scannable Résumé

To accommodate the limited optical character recognition technology associated with typical scanning devices, make sure your résumé text is crystal clear and the letters do not touch one another. While serif fonts such as Bookman, Courier, and Times New Roman are easier for the eye to read, sans serif fonts scan better because they lack the decorative marks at the end of the character strokes. The box on page 12 provides a comparison of fonts.

Avoid using graphics, borders, lines, underlining, shading, boldface type, bullets, italics, brackets, and parentheses. To further minimize the chance of lost content, do not fold a résumé unless the creases avoid the lines of type. If your résumé exceeds one page, include your name on the second page and do not use a staple.

Preparing an Electronic Résumé

The same guidelines outlined for scanned résumés apply when preparing an electronic résumé. Usually, electronic résumés get submitted by e-mail, through a Web page, or by completing an electronic form. Prepare your résumé in plain text using word processing software, and then save the document as "text only" or "rich text format" to eliminate formatting codes and design elements such as boldface and bullets.

To retain some formatting, you can use all capital letters instead of boldface and replace bullets with asterisks. Each line should not exceed 60 characters in length, including spaces and punctuation. Do not use your word processor's word-wrapping feature. Instead put a hard carriage return at the end of each line. This avoids exceeding the line length of a typical computer screen. Use the space bar instead of a tab for spacing.[1]

When sending your résumé as an e-mail attachment, use the ASCII (American Standard Code of Information Interchange) rich text format. Use ASCII hypertext markup language (HTML) format for publishing your résumé on the World Wide Web.

When preparing an electronic résumé, use the Adobe Acrobat portable document format, or PDF file. Using a PDF file you can transmit a document exactly as it was prepared, so a potential employer can view and print it on any system. To prepare PDF files, use Adobe Acrobat software. If you only want to view PDF files without the ability to create them, you can download a free copy of Adobe Reader from www.adobe.com

Regardless of the file type you use, test the appearance of the final copy by sending the completed electronic résumé to your e-mail address.

Keywords

To make electronic and scanned résumés more effective, you may need to include keywords or phrases that match those specified by an employer or program director. Try to include as many keywords as possible when describing your skills and qualifications. You may even want to consider a résumé section listing all keywords, especially those related to skills. Table 2.3 lists common keywords for pharmacy-related electronic résumés.

Reference

1. Criscito P. *Résumés in Cyberspace*. Colorado Springs: ProType, Ltd; 1997: 83.

Chapter 3

Tips, Checklists, and Sample Résumés

When selecting your résumé's content and format, keep in mind what you want to accomplish as well as what the business and professional communities expect. "Anything goes" does not apply. Instead, follow tried-and-true formats and use standard headings and patterns of organization.

This chapter gives examples of effective résumés, tips for format and approach, and advice about problems to avoid. The checklists should help you evaluate your résumé to ensure you've included key elements and haven't made mistakes that will detract from your résumé's success. In addition, Table 3.1 lists commonly used résumé headings and subheadings.

Format

Your résumé format will vary depending on whether you need a standard, scannable, or electronic résumé. Several factors can help make your résumé readable and pleasing to the eye. Use the checklist in the box on the left to ensure you've incorporated the key design elements into your résumé.

The Standard Résumé

Keep a standard résumé as a permanent or hard copy, even if you primarily send out electronic versions. Without the limitations imposed by electronic transmission and scanning, you will have more format flexibility. Even so, adhere to the design guidelines in the box to the right.

Scannable Résumés

To make your résumé suitable for scanning, you will need to alter the format to accommodate the use of optical character recognition technology. The checklist on page 19 lists some general guidelines to follow.

CHECKLIST OF RÉSUMÉ DESIGN ELEMENTS

- Keep the length to one page, and definitely no more than two pages.

- Use a high-quality bond paper in white, off-white, or light ivory.

- Position the watermark, if present, on the top side of the paper for printing.

- Use a quality laser jet printer.

- Use only one side of each page for printing.

- Ensure that typed copy appears symmetrical on the page.

- Achieve a reasonable balance between typed copy and white space to avoid an overcrowded look.

- Maintain one-inch margins at the top, bottom, and sides of the document.

- Justify the left margin.

- Avoid the use of graphics.

CHECKLIST FOR STANDARD RÉSUMÉS

- Choose a consistent serif font (e.g., Bookman Old Style, Courier, Georgia, Times New Roman) or a sans serif font (e.g., Arial, Lucida Sans, Tahoma, Verdana).

- Use a font size between 10 and 14 points.

- Limit the number of font sizes to no more than three.

- Use various design elements (e.g., bullets, lines, italics, boldface type, shading) to create a unique appearance, but do not overuse them.

Information Category	Alternative Headings and Subheadings
Career Goal	goal, objective, career objective, position objective
Summary of Qualifications	profile, qualifications profile, career profile, professional profile, career highlights, professional accomplishments, achievements, key achievements, highlights of achievements, synopsis
Education	academic preparation, educational background, educational and professional training, education and specialized training, education and professional development, academic degrees and postgraduate training
Thesis *(Consider this as a separate heading if thesis is not included in the education section)*	dissertation, dissertation title, master's project
Training *(Consider this as a separate heading if postgraduate training is not included in the education or experience sections)*	specialized training, postgraduate training, residency, residency experience, fellowship, fellowship experience, postdoctoral experience, mentoring
Experience	highlights of experience, employment experience, employment, employment history, work history, professional experience, pharmacy practice experience, professional highlights and achievements, experience and accomplishments, professional background, experience summary *Possible Subheadings:* internships, clerkships (e.g., completed, scheduled), residency rotations (e.g., completed, scheduled, concurrent, longitudinal), experiential learning, professional development, clinical experience, related experience, other work experience, externships (i.e., advanced pharmacy practice experience rotations), positions held
Special Skills	technical skills, technology skills, computer skills, equipment knowledge and skills, computer proficiency, computer software proficiency
Licenses and Certificates *(Include skills that are relevant but outside the general body of pharmacy skills)*	credentials, licenses, licensure, professional licensure, certificates, certifications, licensure and certifications, professional registration, professional certifications, special training
Research Experience	research, grants, contracts, grants and contracts, grants and contracts (approved and funded), grants and contracts, (approved, not funded), research funding applications, grants reviewed, review panel experience, patents, theses committees, dissertation committees, postdoctoral resident supervision, postdoctoral residency preceptorship, postdoctoral residents, postdoctoral fellow supervision, postdoctoral fellows, graduate students supervised, laboratory research experience, clinical research experience, research coordination and direction, research supervision, scholarship, scholarship experience, projects, major research interests, research interests
Academic Appointments	teaching experience, instruction, course participation, courses taught, courses developed, courses developed and taught, graduate course participation, professional course participation, course highlights, areas of expertise, areas of concentration, peer-reviewed continuing education, extramural lecture experience

Information Category	Alternative Headings and Subheadings
Administrative Experience	personnel management, fiscal management, supervisory experience
Publications	recent publications, publications in peer-reviewed journals, selected publications, scholarly works, review articles, monographs *Possible Subheadings:* textbook chapters, books, monographs, books and monographs, articles in refereed journals, editorials, films, audiotapes, computer simulations, self-instructional programs, creative works, bibliographies, review articles, published proceedings, published abstracts, abstracts, manuscripts submitted for publication, editorial boards, editorial activities, journal referee, miscellaneous publications
Presentations	invited presentations, recent presentations, poster presentations, invited lectures, invited papers and lectures, research papers presented at national meetings, seminars presented, scholarly presentations, conference presentations, workshops
Affiliations	memberships, professional memberships, professional affiliations, professional associations, professional and community affiliations, professional societies, membership in professional organizations (Appointments and offices held may be included with the listing of respective affiliations)
Leadership Experience	appointments and offices held, committee leadership, professional association leadership *Possible Subheadings:* name of the affiliation, followed by appointments and offices held
Consulting Experience	consulting, consultation, consulting projects, consultantships, consulting activity
Service Activities	community service, volunteer service, volunteerism, volunteer work, community involvement, community and volunteer activities, academic service, public service, professional service, academic service and committee activity, committee activity (e.g., national, university, school or college, department or division, association)
Professional Development	postgraduate professional development *Possible Subheadings:* continuing education, meetings attended, courses attended, seminars and symposia attended, conferences attended
Military Experience	military service
Awards and Honors	honors and distinctions, distinctions, accomplishments and awards, academic achievements, academic awards, academic honors, special honors, special recognition, selected achievements, awards and fellowships, scholarships, prizes
Personal Interests *(Include these only if they have some uniqueness or bearing on the position)*	leisure activities, sports activities, hobbies
References	

DO'S AND DON'TS OF RÉSUMÉ WRITING

DO:

- Use a consistent format throughout your résumé.

- Use either your full legal name or your first name, middle initial, and last name.

- Arrange experience according to a chronological, functional, or combination format.

- List positions in reverse chronological order according to date.

- Include accurate position titles.

- Use the present tense when describing your current work, and the past tense when describing previous positions.

- Quantify your accomplishments whenever you can (number of procedures, increases in services, amount of budget, etc.).

- Describe skills using phrases with action verbs.

- Emphasize achievements rather than providing a laundry list of duties.

- Consider highlighting special skills with a unique heading.

- Identify the title, sponsor, and date of significant recognition or awards.

- Write out numbers between one and nine, and use numerals for 10 and above.

- Use a consistent format for telephone numbers and dates.

- Use the proper two-letter abbreviations for states.

- Proofread the document for grammar, spelling, syntax, and punctuation errors.

DON'T:

- Put the word "Résumé" as the document's heading.

- Use vague descriptions.

- Exaggerate your responsibilities or accomplishments.

- Use jargon, unfamiliar abbreviations, or slang.

- Allow any typographical, spelling, or grammatical errors.

- List your references on the résumé.

Electronic Résumés

Résumés suitable for sending electronically must get modified even further than scannable résumés because of inconsistencies in hardware components and software programs. The box on the next page lists some guidelines to follow for creating electronic résumés.

Helpful Hints

When you prepare your résumé, follow these guidelines to avoid many common mistakes.

Résumé Headings

Generally, you do not need a heading for your contact information. Depending on the complexity of the information, however, labels can sometimes help. Some examples include:

- Addresses and telephone numbers.

- Permanent address.

- Temporary address.

- Employment address.

- Office.

- Home.

Table 3.1 on pages 16 and 17 lists commonly used résumé headings and subheadings. You can use this list as a guide in selecting the most appropriate headings for your résumé.

Spell Checking

Don't forget to check your document for spelling errors before saving as a text file. Use the "spell check" function on your word processing program, but don't rely on it alone. Read each word carefully.

Proofreading

Before proofreading your own work, put it aside for a day or two. After that, you can read it again with fresh eyes. Some people find it helpful to proofread backwards, starting with the last word and moving in reverse order to the first word. Or, you can ask a friend or colleague to proofread your résumé for you. Pay special attention to headings, since most errors in this area get overlooked.

Sample Résumés

On the following pages you'll find examples of résumés for pharmacy professionals, with comments about their features. Although good résumés follow certain general rules, there are no absolutes, and no particular style is right for everyone.

The most important thing is to make sure your résumé lets your strengths shine through. In the 15 seconds or so that decision makers—whether pharmacists or human resources specialists—spend skimming each applicant's materials to decide whether to consider him or her for an interview, will they be able to identify substantive skills and achievements?

A final word of caution about résumés: always be truthful. Although you need to portray yourself in the best possible light, saying you directed a blood pressure screening when all you did was show up and watch, or published a paper that doesn't even exist, will come back to haunt you in the interview.

> **TIP:** Use design elements such as boldface type, bullets, lines, and italics judiciously. Do not use graphics in your résumé. And most importantly, make sure your résumé has no typographical, grammatical, or spelling errors.

CHECKLIST FOR ELECTRONIC RÉSUMÉS

In addition to using the guidelines provided for scannable résumés, when preparing an electronic résumé make sure to:

- Use capital letters as a replacement for boldface type or underlining in heads and subheads.

- Save the final document in a suitable format for electronic transmission (e.g., HTML for Web posting and ASCII or PDF for attaching to e-mail).

CHECKLIST FOR SCANNABLE RÉSUMÉS

- Choose a consistent sans serif font.

- Avoid folding and stapling the résumé.

- Save the final document as a "text only," "rich text format," or "PDF" file.

- Minimize the use of design elements (e.g., bullets, lines, underlining, italics, boldface type, brackets, parentheses, shading).

- Create spaces using the spacebar and avoid the use of tabs.

- Use hard carriage returns at the end of each line.

- Do not use word wrapping.

- Include key words related to the skills included in a computer search strategy (see Table 2.4).

- Use a font size between 12 and 14 points.

- Include your name on the second page.

- Maintain one-inch margins at the top, bottom, and sides of the document.

- Justify the left margin.

- Avoid the use of graphics.

A chronological résumé for a pharmacy technician and chemistry student looking for a position in a community pharmacy. Font: Times New Roman 12 point.

Objective helps employers focus quickly on what this candidate is looking for.

Ashley Brooke Foster

Local Address	Permanent Address
9501 Rio Verde Way	3301 Thorntree Road
Tucson, Arizona 85710	Scottsville, Arizona 85260
(480) 451-8142	(520) 290-7721
E-mail: abfoster@u.arizona.edu	

OBJECTIVE: Pharmacy technician position in a community pharmacy where I can apply my customer-service skills and knowledge of pharmacy practice and terminology.

EDUCATION: University of Arizona — August 2004 – Present
Tucson, Arizona — Anticipated Graduation: 2008
Major: Chemistry — G.P.A.: 3.4 / 4.0

Chaparral High School — September 2000 – May 2004
Scottsville, Arizona

EXPERIENCE: Receptionist, Hazleton Realtors — June 2004 – August 2004
Scottsville, Arizona
Achievements: Received special
award for exceptional customer relations

Does an effective job of concisely highlighting achievements.

Sales Associate, Johnson Floral Designs — May 2003 – August 2003
Scottsville, Arizona
Achievements: Developed flyers and coupons
to target prom and graduation business

Lifeguard, Verda Country Club — June 2002 – August 2002
Scottsville, Arizona
Achievements: Planned/taught 6 a.m. water
aerobics class for senior citizens 3 days/week:
improved pool maintenance procedures

Volunteer, Mary Immaculate Hospital — July 2001 – December 2003
Scottsville, Arizona
(4-20 Hours/Week)
Achievements: Spent 4-20 hours/week helping
to orient patients and families to hospital services

CERTIFICATES: American Red Cross First Aid Certificate — 2002 – 2005
American Red Cross Adult CPR Certificate — 2002 – 2005
American Red Cross Infant & Child CPR — 2002 – 2005

MEMBERSHIPS: Affiliate of the American Chemical Society — 2004 – Present
Chemistry Club, University of Arizona — 2005 – Present

LANGUAGES: Fluent in English and Spanish.

If you speak multiple languages it is useful to say so.

Actual résumé size is 8.5 x 11

A chronological résumé for a pharmacy technician attending college part time.
Font: Arial Narrow 12 and 10 point.

Page A. Shaw
3321 Guyton Way, Apartment 32A
Jacksonville, Florida 32225
904/645-9729

Format is simple and clean.

EDUCATION

September 2001 – Present
(Part-time)

University of North Florida
College of Arts and Sciences
Jacksonville, Florida
Completed 44 Semester Hours

September 1997 – May 2001

Providence High School
Jacksonville, Florida

Here she lists positions held and general duties. More emphasis on key achievements would help employers quickly identify what strengths she offers them.

WORK EXPERIENCE

July 2001 – Present

Eckerd Pharmacy, Jacksonville, FL
Pharmacy Technician
Assist pharmacists in dispensing an average of 250 prescription medications daily; place orders; create reports; train new technicians; update computer records

May 2000 – August 2000

Sunshine Gallery, Inc., Atlantic Beach, FL
Customer Service Clerk
Sold, matted, and framed artwork

May 1999 – August 1999

Jackson and Associates, Atlantic Beach, FL
Secretarial Assistant
Performed administrative tasks; revamped customer files

May 1998 – September 1998

Leed's Department Store, Jacksonville, FL
Sales Associate
Sold children's clothing; exceeded monthly sales goals

COMPUTER SKILLS

Microsoft Windows, Word, Excel, Access, WordPerfect

ORGANIZATIONS

January 2002 – Present

Pre-Medical Profession's Program
University of North Florida

References Available on Request

Including this statement is optional and can easily be omitted if you need space for more critical information.

Actual résumé size is 8.5 x 11

Chronological résumé of a certified pharmacy technician enrolled in a pre-pharmacy course of study. Font: Arial 12 point.

Objective is concise and direct.

MICHAEL PATRICK GARRETT

804-A Westside Avenue • Iowa City, Iowa 52240 • 319.358.5107
E-mail: mpgarret@uiowa.edu

OBJECTIVE	Pharmacy technician position in a health-system pharmacy	
EDUCATION	August 2004 - Present	University of Iowa Iowa City, Iowa Major: Pre-Pharmacy
	June 2003 – May 2004	Grand View College Des Moines, Iowa Pharmacy Technician Diploma Program
WORK EXPERIENCE	JUNE 2004 – AUGUST 2004	PHARMACY TECHNICIAN Albertson's Pharmacy Des Moines, Iowa
	May 1999 – August 2003 (Summers)	Groundskeeper Deer Valley Golf Club Des Moines, Iowa
CERTIFICATION	Certified Pharmacy Technician (CPhT) awarded July 2004	
HONORS	Dean's List, Grand View College, Spring 2004 Eagle Scout, Mid-Iowa Council, 2001	

This résumé has plenty of extra space to include a few key duties and accomplishments. Readers get no sense of this candidate's top attributes. Being a groundskeeper, for example, may call for initiative and problem-solving skills.

Pay attention to details. The font switch here is inconsistent with the rest of the format.

These honors suggest he has leadership abilities, but the candidate misses the opportunity to elaborate.

Actual résumé size is 8.5 x 11

Chronological résumé of a pharmacy technician who wants to attend pharmacy school.
Font: Times New Roman 12 point.

MINH T. NGO

5231 Warfield Drive
Oakland, California 94611
(510) 339-5416

This person seems to have a lot of initiative the résumé does not showcase by merely listing jobs and volunteer work.

_____OBJECTIVE_____

To gain admission to College of Pharmacy at Western University of Health Sciences.

_____EXPERIENCE_____

June 2004 – Present	Pharmacy Technician	Bayside Pharmacy Oakland, CA
May 2003 – August 2003	Pharmacy Technician	Providence Hospital Oakland, CA
June 2002 – August 2002	Bank Teller	Wells Fargo Bank Berkeley, CA
July 2000 – December 2003	Waiter / Cook	Great Wall Restaurant Berkeley, CA

_____EDUCATION_____

September 2000 – June 2004	Freemont High School Oakland, California	Diploma

_____CERTIFICATES_____

As shown here, certification can be a separate category.

2003 – Present	Certified Pharmacy Technician	Successfully Completed Pharmacy Technician Certification Board Exam

_____COMMUNITY SERVICE_____

January 2002 – Present	Volunteer	Metropolitan Area Food Bank Oakland, CA

Actual résumé size is 8.5 x 11

Two-page chronological résumé of a student seeking a pharmacy internship. Font: Garamond 11 point.

Lia Kim Chang

The objective and summary statement play up her skills.

1571 Camellia Drive
San Francisco, California 94122

Telephone: 415.566.8507
E-mail: chang525@aol.com

CAREER OBJECTIVE

To obtain a pharmacy internship that builds on my strengths, expands my knowledge, and allows me to contribute to the organization's goals.

PROFESSIONAL SUMMARY

Pharmacy intern with excellent interpersonal, leadership, and organizational skills. Background in research, patient education, and pharmacy practice.

EDUCATION

University of California at San Francisco
School of Pharmacy
San Francisco, California

2004 – Present
Degree anticipated May 2006

Santa Clara University
Santa Clara, California

2000 – 2004
B.S. in Biology

The way she spotlights her achievements lets readers know she is someone who gets things done.

PROFESSIONAL EXPERIENCE

Pharmacy Technician, St. John's Medical Center
San Francisco, California

2004 – Present
(Part-time)

- Conducted in-store study with over 100 patients, comparing effectiveness of web-based tools to communicate information about drug therapy and drug interactions

- Organized and updated records from pharmacists' patient counseling sessions

- Presented information sessions for senior patients on new drug therapies and generic options for treatment

- Initiated and organized quarterly monthly "brown bag" sessions in the Medical Center's cafeteria in which pharmacists to review prescription medications of seniors

Lia Kim Chang (Page 2) ←

Although many people do not use two-page résumés until they have many years of work experience, this résumé contains good information and would be too cramped on one page.

PROFESSIONAL EXPERIENCE (Continued)

Pharmacy Technician, Longs Drugs   2002 – 2003
Santa Clara, California   (Summer)

- Researched and recommended support groups for patients with ongoing medication needs and medical conditions, including asthma, diabetes, allergies, and osteoporosis

- Evaluated options for updating telephone system to make requesting prescription refills easier for patients

- Collaborated with two other technicians to publicize expanded wellness programs

Laboratory Assistant I   2002 – 2003
Biology Department   (Summer)
Santa Clara University

- Inventoried and reordered supplies and maintained stock records for department chair

- Mentored students in two sections of Introduction to Biology summer course

MEMBERSHIPS

Academy of Students of Pharmacy of the   2004 – Present
  American Pharmacists Association (APhA-ASP)
California Pharmacists Association   2004 – Present

AWARDS AND HONORS

APhA-ASP Chapter Vice President   2005

Chair, Operation Diabetes Campaign promoting   2005
  early screening and detection

Poster Presentation, Diabetes Awareness, APhA-ASP   2005
  Region 8 Midyear Meeting, October 14-16, Las Vegas

Service Award, Friend to Friend, for leading drive to   2004
  supply wigs and scarves to low-income cancer patients

Beta Beta Beta National Biological Honor Society   2003 – 2004

Dean's List, College of Arts and Sciences   2001 – 2004
Santa Clara University

This combination résumé for a pharmacy student has a particularly attractive format.
Font: Georgia 11 and 10 point.

Amanda Ashley Sanderson
4145 Alton Lane
Denver, Colorado 80249
303.375.8019
303.237.8754 (Cellular)
amanda.sanderson@uchsc.edu

> *Résumé may have been prepared for distribution at a job fair, since it lacks an objective. When you are applying for a specific opportunity, tailor your objective to match.*

EDUCATION

University of Colorado Health Sciences Center   August 2003 - Present
School of Pharmacy, Denver, Colorado
Doctor of Pharmacy degree anticipated, May 2007

University of Colorado   September 1999 - June 2003
Boulder, Colorado
B.S. in Biochemistry

EXPERIENCE

Pharmacy Technician   June 2003 - August 2004
Walgreens, Denver, Colorado   (Summers)
Supervisor: Debra A. Ferrell, R.Ph.
    Key responsibilities: Assisted the pharmacist in preparing
    prescription medications for dispensing, processed insurance
    claims, maintained an inventory for prescription drug products,
    nonprescription drug products, and medical devices

> *Listing supervisors is a convention seen on many pharmacy résumés. It's a plus when the supervisor is a known leader or innovator in pharmacy.*

Research Assistant   June 2002 - August 2002
Department of Chemistry, University of Colorado at Boulder
Advisor: Joseph N. Shockley, Ph.D.
    Key responsibilities: Assisted with biochemical and
    biophysical studies of sensory receptors and signaling proteins

Receptionist   May 2001 - August 2001
Steven V. Edmonds, M.D., Grand Junction, Colorado
Supervisor: Nancy Holmes
    Key responsibilities: Arranged appointments for patients,
    ordered office supplies, and performed clerical duties

COMMUNITY SERVICE

Volunteer   June 1998 - August 1998
Memorial Hospital, Grand Junction, Colorado
    Key Activities: Delivered meals to patients, measured
    blood pressures in a diabetes screening clinic, helped
    coordinate community blood drive

AMANDA ASHLEY SANDERSON (Page 2)

CERTIFICATION AND LICENSURE

Pharmacy Intern No. 762 Colorado Board of Pharmacy	May 2004
Certificate of Occupational Proficiency in Emergency Medical Technology Colorado Mountain College Glenwood Springs, Colorado	July 2001

MEMBERSHIPS AND ACTIVITIES

Academy of Students of Pharmacy,   2003 - Present
American Pharmacists Association
    • Co-Chair, Campus Health Fair, Spring 2005
    • Community Immunization Campaign Assistant, 2004

Colorado Society of Health-System Pharmacists,   2004 - Present
Student Chapter
    • Student Representative to Health Sciences Council,
      2005 - 2006

Ski and Snowboard Club,   2000 - 2003
University of Colorado at Boulder
    • Treasurer, 2002 - 2003
    • Activity Committee Chair, 2001 - 2002

An electronic version of this résumé will be provided upon request.

Electronic version of résumé 6. Font: Tahoma 12 and 10 point.

AMANDA ASHLEY SANDERSON

ADDRESS

4145 Alton Lane
Denver, Colorado 80249
303.375.8019
303.237.8754, Cellular
amanda.sanderson@uchsc.edu

EDUCATION

University of Colorado Health Sciences Center
School of Pharmacy, Denver, Colorado
August 2003 – Present
Doctor of Pharmacy degree anticipated May 2007

University of Colorado
Boulder, Colorado
September 1999 – June 2003
B.S. in Biochemistry

EXPERIENCE

Pharmacy Technician
Walgreens, Denver, Colorado
Supervisor: Debra A. Ferrell, R.Ph.
June 2003 – August 2004 (Summers)
Key responsibilities: Assisted the pharmacist in preparing
prescription medications for dispensing, processed insurance
claims, maintained an inventory for prescription drug products,
nonprescription drug products, and medical devices

Research Assistant
Department of Chemistry, University of Colorado at Boulder
Advisor: Joseph N. Shockley, Ph.D.
June 2002 – August 2002
Key responsibilities: Assisted with biochemical and biophysical
studies of sensory receptors and signaling proteins

Receptionist
Steven V. Edmonds, M.D., Grand Junction, Colorado
Supervisor: Nancy Holmes
May 2001 – August 2001
Key responsibilities: Arranged appointments for patients, ordered
office supplies, and performed general clerical duties

AMANDA ASHLEY SANDERSON, Page 2

COMMUNITY SERVICE

Volunteer
Memorial Hospital, Grand Junction, Colorado
June 1998 – August 1998
Key Activities: Delivered meals to patients, measured blood pressures
in a diabetes screening clinic, helped coordinate community blood drive

CERTIFICATION AND LICENSURE

Pharmacy Intern No. 762
Colorado Board of Pharmacy
May 2004

Certificate of Occupational Proficiency
in Emergency Medical Technology
Colorado Mountain College
Glenwood Springs, Colorado
July 2001

MEMBERSHIPS

American Pharmacists Association,
Academy of Students of Pharmacy
2003 – Present
--Co-Chair, Campus Health Fair, Spring 2005
--Community Immunization Campaign Assistant, 2004

Colorado Society of Health-System Pharmacists
Student Chapter, 2004 – Present
--Student Representative to Health Sciences Council, 2005 – 2006

Ski and Snowboard Club, University of Colorado
at Boulder, 2000 – 2003
--Treasurer, 2002 – 2003
--Activity Committee Chair, 2001 – 2002

A chronological résumé for a graduating pharmacy student.
Font: Verdana 11 point.

Concise and easy to skim, this résumé gives the most essential data. It could expand on the candidate's achievements and leadership experience.

Ronald James Harrison

2910 Roswell Terrace	Atlanta, Georgia 30303	(404) 220-5001
	rjharris@peachnet.com	

Objective   To obtain a community pharmacy practice residency.

Education

Mercer University	2002 - Present
Southern School of Pharmacy	Pharm.D. Candidate, 2006
Atlanta, Georgia	Cumulative G.P.A.: 3.4 /4.0
Macon State College	1999 - 2002
Macon, Georgia	Pre-Pharmacy Curriculum

Experience

Pharmacy Intern	October 2003 - Present
CVS Pharmacy	
Atlanta, Georgia	
Emergency Room Technician	June 2001 - August 2002
Medical Center of Central Georgia	(Part-time)
Macon, Georgia	

Licenses

Georgia Board of Pharmacy	April 2003
Internship License # 1059	

Awards and Recognition

Phi Lambda Sigma Leadership Society	2004 - Present
School of Pharmacy Dean's List	Fall Semesters, 2003 and 2004
A.T. Simpson Scholarship Award	2003

Professional Affiliations

Student National Pharmaceutical Association	2002 - Present

- President, 2003 - 2004
- Treasurer, 2002 - 2003

Academy of Students of Pharmacy	2002 - Present

- 2004 Delegate, Annual Convention

American Pharmacists Association	2002 - Present

Résumé of a pharmacist who has completed residency training. Font: Lucida Sans 11 point.

> *An objective, although not essential, would help readers understand what sort of position he is looking for.*

Kenneth R. Crow
2331 Marsh Street
Oklahoma City, Oklahoma 73159
(405) 688-2091
Kenneth.Crow@med.va.gov

QUALIFICATIONS SUMMARY

Doctor of Pharmacy licensed in Texas and Oklahoma, with two years of hospital pharmacy residency training. Experience in interdisciplinary collaboration, pharmaceutical care, chronic disease management, and emergency cardiac care. Knowledge of complex delivery systems, investigational drugs, natural products, emerging medications, and electronic prescribing and medical records. Committed to cutting-edge practice and positive patient outcomes.

> *This summary gives a snapshot of the candidate's strengths. A problem, however, is that the information is not fully supported by what appears in the body of the résumé. Also, this font is hard to read in paragraph format.*

EDUCATION

Doctor of Pharmacy
2001 – 2003

University of Texas
San Antonio, Texas

Bachelor of Science in Pharmacy
1998 – 2001

University of Oklahoma
Oklahoma City, Oklahoma

Pre-Pharmacy Curriculum
1996 – 1998

University of Oklahoma
Norman, Oklahoma

PROFESSIONAL TRAINING

Specialized Residency in Primary Care
Pharmacy Practice
2004 – 2005

University of Oklahoma College
of Pharmacy and Veterans Affairs
Medical Center

Residency in Pharmacy Practice
2003 – 2004

Integris Baptist Medical Center
Oklahoma City, Oklahoma

LICENSES AND CERTIFICATES

Pharmacist No. 3065 (2001)
Pharmacist No. 1764 (2001)
Advanced Cardiac Life Support Provider (2004)

Texas State Board of Pharmacy
Oklahoma State Board of Pharmacy
American Heart Association

AWARDS AND HONORS – UNIVERSITY OF OKLAHOMA

Rho Chi Academic Honor Society, Gamma Chapter, 2000
Phi Lambda Sigma, National Pharmacy Leadership Society, Alpha Epsilon, 2001
Dean's List, 1998 – 2001

PROFESSIONAL MEMBERSHIPS

Oklahoma Society of Health-System Pharmacists
American Society of Health-System Pharmacists
American Pharmacists Association
American College of Clinical Pharmacy

> *A bare bones list that is easy to skim, but it fails to highlight unique experiences and achievements that set this candidate apart from others.*

Actual résumé size is 8.5 x 11

This two-page chronological résumé shows a variety of professional experience.
Font: Century Schoolbook 11 and 10 point.

Summary gives readers a preview of information in the body of the résumé.

Kirit Raman Patel

9086 Haywood Street
Philadelphia, Pennsylvania 19120

Telephone ■ (215) 276-2492
Telepage ■ (215) 582-8067
E-mail ■ krpatel@mindspring.com

Summary

Newly licensed pharmacist with experience providing highly skilled services in community and hospital pharmacies and in manufacturing. Demonstrated leadership and communication through organizing and delivering community health campaigns, patient education, and staff presentations.

Education

1999 – 2005	University of Sciences in Philadelphia Philadelphia College of Pharmacy Philadelphia, Pennsylvania	Doctor of Pharmacy 2005

Useful details are provided here.

Professional Experience and Achievements

Summers 2003 and 2004	SmithKline Beecham Philadelphia, Pennsylvania	Quality Control Technician

Ensured compliance with rigorous quality standards through inspection and statistical sampling. Audited productivity statistics from peers during mandatory review cycles. Prepared and gave staff presentations on quality control advances.

Summer 2002	Rite Aid Pharmacy Philadelphia, Pennsylvania	Pharmacy Intern

Assisted two pharmacists in filling more than 2000 prescriptions per week. Reduced inventory carrying costs by 10% by conscientiously controlling prescription drug inventory.

Summer 2001	St. Luke's Hospital Harrisburg, Pennsylvania	Pharmacy Intern

Managed medication counseling center for low-income patients. Wrote and designed patient checklists and information sheets. Scheduled pharmacists and physicians for counseling sessions. Maintained records for patients and reviewed recommendations for potential medication interactions.

Summer 2000	Rite Aid Pharmacy Harrisburg, Pennsylvania	Pharmacy Intern

Assisted in routine prescription processing. Processed prescription insurance claims. Developed fact sheet and flyer for blood pressure screenings.

1997 – 1999 (Part-time)	Mitchell's Apothecary Harrisburg, Pennsylvania	Clerk

Interacted with clients, responded to inquiries, placed orders for supplies, helped maintain records and files.

Licenses

2000	Pennsylvania State Board of Pharmacy	Intern
2005	Pennsylvania State Board of Pharmacy	Pharmacists

Actual résumé size is 8.5 x 11

Kirit Raman Patel   Page 2

Recognition and Awards

University of the Sciences in Philadelphia
2005	▪ Community Service Award
2004	▪ William P. Johnson Scholarship
2004	▪ Patient Counseling Competition Winner
2003	▪ Rho Chi Academic Honor Society, Alpha Tau Chapter
2002	▪ Dr. James R. Mitchell Scholarship

SmithKline Beecham
2003	▪ Employee of the Month, Quality Control Section Beecham

Memberships

2004 – 2005	Student Government Association, University of Sciences ▪ Vice-President of Activities
2003 – Present	Pennsylvania Society of Health-System Pharmacists ▪ Member, Legislative Affairs Committee (2002 – 2003)
2002 – Present	Phi Delta Chi Fraternity
2001 – Present	Academy of Students of Pharmacy, American Pharmacists Association ▪ Coordinator, Professional Projects (2003 – 2004) ▪ Treasurer (2002 – 2003) ▪ Member, Legislative Affairs Committee (2001 – 2002)
2001 – Present	Pennsylvania Society of Health-System Pharmacists ▪ Member, Legislative Affairs Committee (2002 – 2003)

Computer Skills

Software Proficiency
- ▪ Microsoft Word, Excel, Access, PowerPoint
- ▪ Corel WordPerfect

Desktop Publishing
- ▪ Microsoft FrontPage
- ▪ JAVA Script
- ▪ Hypertext Markup Language

Service Activities

Academy of Students of Pharmacy
2004	▪ Diabetes Screening Campaign Chairman
2004	▪ "Flu Shot" Campaign Committee Member
2003	▪ Blood Pressure Screening Coordinator
2002	▪ Alzheimer's Association Memory Walk, Participant
2001	▪ Blood Pressure Screening Committee Member

Phi Delta Chi Professional Pharmacy Fraternity
2004	▪ Thanksgiving Food Drive Coordinator

A functional or skills résumé for a home infusion pharmacist, formerly a nurse. Font: Arial 12 point.

Gina Maria Ruiz
6105 Fulton Way, Lubbock, Texas 79410 • 806-795-6212 • GRuiz@aol.com

CAREER PROFILE
- Twenty years' experience with healthcare education and practice
- Eleven years' experience as a practicing registered pharmacist
- Two years' experience as a practicing registered nurse
- Excellent interpersonal communication and team-building skills
- Certified diabetic educator

Career profile encapsulates key details.

HIGHLIGHTS OF PROFESSIONAL EXPERIENCE

Pharmacy Practice
- Designed content for bimonthly staff training in both community and hospital settings
- Trained staff of 20 on protocols for home infusion pharmacy practice
- Supervised and mentored pharmacy interns and clerkship students
- Managed the JCAHO accreditation process for a home infusion therapy service
- Achieved 80% patient compliance rating for diabetic patients in educational study evaluating the effectiveness of a pilot infusion pump for insulin therapy

Nursing Practice
- Cared for patients in both ambulatory care and inpatient settings
- Facilitated prenatal counseling sessions in a prenatal care clinic for over 250 clients

EMPLOYMENT HISTORY

Johnson's Pharmacy and Home Infusion Services, Abilene, Texas
- Director of Pharmacy, Home Infusion Services, 2000 - Present
- Pharmacist-in-Charge, 1998 - 2000
- Staff Pharmacist, 1994 - 1998

St. Vincent's Hospital, Abilene, Texas
- Staff Nurse, 1983 - 1985

Highlights listed here call employers' attention to strengths and away from employment gaps.

EDUCATION

University of Houston College of Pharmacy, Houston, Texas
Bachelor of Science in Pharmacy, degree conferred 1994

Hardin-Simmons University, Abilene, Texas
Pre-Pharmacy Curriculum, 1989 - 1991

St. Vincent's Hospital School of Nursing, Abilene, Texas
Diploma in Nursing, awarded 1983

Résumé of someone in academia. This person most likely uses a CV more often than a résumé, but it's good to have both. Font: Times New Roman 12 point.

A summary or objective would help readers understand her specific strengths and what she is looking for.

Valerie Nga Tran

CONTACT INFORMATION

University Address:

Department of Pharmaceutical Sciences
The University of Connecticut
School of Pharmacy, U-84
Storrs, CT 06269-8320
Phone: 860-486-3285
E-mail: vnt97003@uconnvm.uconn.edu

Home Address:

2313 Wildwood Way
Storrs, CT 06268
Phone: 860-429-6679
E-mail: vntran5@hotmail.com

EDUCATION

University of Connecticut
School of Pharmacy
Storrs, Connecticut

Ph.D. in Pharmaceutical Sciences
Pharmaceutics Concentration
August 2002 - Present
Degree anticipated, May 2006
Major Advisor: Harold J. Lee, Ph.D.

Rutgers University
College of Pharmacy
Piscataway, New Jersey

B.S. in Pharmacy with Distinction
Degree Conferred, May 2002

The facts of her background are listed in a clear, concise way.

TEACHING EXPERIENCE

Graduate Teaching Assistant

Pharmacy 209 (Physicochemical Principles of Drugs, 1 Semester Hour, Laboratory, Fall Semesters, 2003 - 2005)

Lecturer and Tutor

Pharmacy 208 and 210 (Physicochemical Principles of Drugs I and II, 3 Semester Hours, Fall and Spring Semesters, 2003 - 2005)

RESEARCH EXPERIENCE

M.S. Thesis

The Effects of Temperature and Moisture on the Stability of Freeze-Dried Prostaglandin E1

Ph.D. Thesis

Diode Laser Induced Fluorescence Detection of Daunorubicin in Plasma Using Pressurized Electrochromatography

Valerie Nga Tran   Page 2

SELECTED PUBLICATIONS

Tran VN, Lee HJ, Freisen TY. The effects of temperature and moisture on the stability of freeze-dried prostaglandin E1. *Biopharmaceutics and Drug Dispos* 2003;23:213-217.

Tran VN, Watson FN, Tyler AB, Lee HJ. Diode Laser Induced Fluoresence Detection of Daunorubicin in Plasma. *J Pharm Sci* 2006; In Press.

AFFILIATIONS

2001 – Present	American Pharmacists Association
2002 – Present	Connecticut Pharmacists Association
2003 – Present	Student Chapter of the American Association of Pharmaceutical Scientists

AWARDS AND HONORS

2004	Pre-Doctoral Fellowship, American Foundation for Pharmaceutical Education
2002	S.W. Higgins Scholarship Award, Rutgers University College of Pharmacy
2000	Rho Chi Honor Society, Alpha Eta Chapter, Rutgers University
2000	Who's Who Among Students in American Universities and Colleges
1997 – 2002	Dean's List, Rutgers University College of Pharmacy (All semesters)

Résumé of a pharmacist/attorney working in the pharmaceutical industry. Font: Arial 12 point.

Eduardo Antonio Foster

Department of Regulatory Affairs
PharmaMedica, Inc.
3 Langford Parkway
Wallingford, CT 06492
(203) 564-7820
fosterea@pm.com

942 Derbyshire Court
Middletown, Connecticut 06457
(860) 447-6720
fosterea@execulink.net

Summary highlights his unique attributes.

PROFESSIONAL SUMMARY

Licensed pharmacist/attorney with 20 years' experience in drug regulation, budget administration, department and project management, and service delivery. Extensive leadership in presentation, interpersonal, and team-building skills. Established track record of meeting and exceeding established goals related to management, training, and education. Bilingual, Spanish and English.

EDUCATION

Juris Doctor, University of Arizona, Tucson	1989 - 1992
B.S. in Pharmacy, University of Arizona, Tucson	1981 - 1986

The way he uses numbers to emphasize responsibilities and achievements is effective.

PROFESSIONAL EXPERIENCE

Director of Regulatory Affairs   2001 - Present
PharmaMedica, Inc., Wallingford, CT

- Spearhead development and implementation of regulatory policies and procedures for licensure of Respitoria®
- Review and execute over 10 investigational drug applications, new drug applications, and abbreviated new drug applications yearly
- Interpret and apply all regulations and guidelines of the Food and Drug Administration concerning drug development
- Prepare and implement annual strategic plan for department of over 75 employees
- Allocate and coordinate departmental resources

Clinical Science Manager   1996 - 2001
Invion Biologicals, San Francisco, CA

- Enhanced client relations as liaison for communicating medical and scientific data
- Led and facilitated biweekly workflow planning and review seminars
- Organized monthly multidisciplinary work sessions to develop cross-functional team expertise
- Screened and updated drug development and clinical research procedures weekly
- Maintained open and positive communications with regulatory authorities

Eduardo Antonio Foster   Page 2

PROFESSIONAL EXPERIENCE (Continued)

Clinical Research Associate II   1992 - 1996
Stratton Pharmaceuticals, La Jolla, CA

- Coordinated and supervised initiation, execution. and analysis of clinical studies of three investigational drugs
- Mentored and supervised 18 Clinical Research Assistants
- Evaluated and selected over 15 Contract Research Organizations yearly
- Arranged and conducted monthly investigator meetings
- Researched and strengthened knowledge in clinical areas of diabetes and infectious disease

Pharmacist (Part-time)   1989 - 1991
Thompson Apothecary, Scottsdale, AZ

- Received and assessed written prescriptions from over 200 prescribers monthly
- Maintained over 500 patient profiles detailing prescription and nonprescription medications and major health conditions
- Delivered and interpreted drug information to prescribers and patients

Pharmaceutical Sales Representative   1986 - 1989
J. H. Downing Company, Phoenix, AZ

Accomplished over 100 calls per month to practicing physicians, pharmacists, hospitals, and other health-related organizations
Provided information about 24 drug products marketed by J. H. Downing Company
Completed two-year training in sales strategies and skills

PROFESSIONAL CREDENTIALS

State Bar of Arizona, Admission   1992
Arizona Board of Pharmacy, License 8875   1986

PROFESSIONAL AND COMMUNITY AFFILIATIONS

American Society for Pharmacy Law   1999 - Present
Rotary International Service Organization   1996 - Present
Arizona Pharmaceutical Association   1983 - Present
American Pharmacists Association   1983 - Present

AWARDS AND RECOGNITION

Community Service Achievement Award   2001
Invion Biologicals

Rotary Volunteers Certificate of Recognition 2000
San Francisco-area Rotary Club

Résumé of a pharmacist practicing in a large corporation. Font: Century Gothic 11 point.

Gerald Gregory Schmidt

4085 Miami Lakes Drive   **(305) 620-8642**
Hialeah, Florida 33014   **ggs007@yahoo.com**

EDUCATION

1986 – 1989	University of Florida College of Pharmacy Gainesville, Florida Bachelor of Science degree in Pharmacy
1983 – 1986	Stetson University DeLand, Florida Pre-pharmacy curriculum

This space could be better used to highlight skills and achievements rather than listing each location. A very sketchy résumé.

EMPLOYMENT

2003 – Present	Pharmacist, Walgreens Company • 830 Miami Lakes Drive, Hialeah, Florida
1989 – 2003	Pharmacist, Eckerd Corporation • 15585 Miami Lakes Drive, Hialeah, Florida • 8842 Golden Gate Parkway, Naples, Florida • 1868 Immokalee Road, Naples, Florida • 2635 Tamiami Trail, Port Charlotte, Florida • 8335 West Water Avenue, Tampa, Florida • 6220 North Florida Avenue, Tampa, Florida

LICENSURE

1989 – Present	Pharmacist (License # PS20376, June 30, 1989) Florida Board of Pharmacy

PROFESSIONAL MEMBERSHIPS

1989 – Present	Florida Pharmacy Association
1989 – Present	American Pharmacists Association

REFERENCES

Available upon request

Actual résumé size is 8.5 x 11

Chronological résumé of a health-system pharmacist.
Font: Times New Roman 11 point.

Summary is helpful, but its content is not fully backed up by the descriptions of his experience below.

Mark Alan Chandler

Professional Summary

Hospital pharmacist with more than 25 years' experience, primarily in the VA system, and instructor of technicians and students of pharmacy and nursing. Broad experience addressing medication needs of hospitalized patients including preparing IV and unit dose medications, drug information, drug interaction monitoring, nutritional services, antibiotic dosing and selection, and inventory management.

Contact Information

Home:

25816 Park Hills Ave, South Holland, Illinois 60615
(708) 368-4219; chand282@excite.com

Work:

Pharmacy Service (119), Edward Hines Jr. VA Hospital
5th Avenue and Roosevelt Road, Hines, Illinois 60141
(708) 202-1872; machan@mail.va.gov

Education

1971 – 1976

Purdue University
School of Pharmacy and Pharmacal Sciences
West Lafayette, Indiana
Bachelor of Science Degree, Pharmacy

Work Experience

1987 – Present

Edward Hines Jr. VA Hospital, Hines, Illinois
Pharmacist, Pharmacy Service

1983 – 1987

Spokane VA Medical Center, Spokane, Washington
Pharmacist, Pharmacy Service

1976 – 1983

Mount Carmel Hospital, Columbus, Ohio
Pharmacist, Department of Pharmacy Services

Teaching Experience

1999 – Present

South Suburban College, South Holland, Illinois
Instructor, Pharmacy Technician Program

1984 – 1987

Washington State University College of Pharmacy
Pullman, Washington
Instructor, Pharmacy Externship Program

1980 – 1983

Mount Carmel Hospital School of Nursing
Columbus, Ohio
Instructor, Pharmacology and Nursing Calculations

Professional Affiliations

1990 – Present

Illinois Council of Health-System Pharmacists
- Treasurer, 2003 – Present
- Organizational Affairs Committee, 1998-2003

1981 – Present

American Society of Health-System Pharmacists

1976 – Present

Purdue Pharmacy Alumni Association

Actual résumé size is 8.5 x 11

Chapter 4

Preparing the Curriculum Vitae

A curriculum vitae or CV outlines your personal background, education, and experience. Unlike a résumé, a CV provides more comprehensive information and usually exceeds one or two pages. Many health professionals, academics, and people in other specialized professions, such as law and engineering, prefer CVs because they contain additional detail about qualifications and activities.

In the pharmacy field, CVs routinely accompany applications for admission to graduate and professional degree programs, employment, internships, postgraduate residencies, fellowships, consulting positions, and organizational leadership positions, as well as grant proposals and nominations for honors and awards.

In contrast, a résumé briefly summarizes the same information and gets used primarily when applying for a specific employment opportunity. When they expect a large applicant pool, potential employers prefer résumés because they can skim them more quickly.

Most health professionals prepare both a résumé and curriculum vitae, since they accommodate differing needs.

Preparing the Curriculum Vitae

The process of preparing the curriculum vitae involves the identical principles as a résumé: presenting your education, experience, and accomplishments clearly and concisely. Because you do not need to restrict the document's length, however, you can provide more complete information and include additional category headings. The box on the following page contains a list of typical categories found on a CV.

Since a curriculum vitae should highlight your strengths, you can include any number of other categories, such as leadership experience, military background, special skills, or consulting experience. The order of the sections and the actual titles you give them will vary on an individual basis. Traditionally, pharmacy professionals place their education before their professional experience.

Personal Information

A CV usually begins with "Curriculum Vitae" at the top of the first page, followed by your full legal name or first name, middle initial, and last name. Next, list personal information such as a temporary and permanent address, telephone number, and e-mail address. You can present this information directly under your name or organize it under a heading such as "personal information" or "contact information."

As explained in Chapter 2, many people include personal information on their CV that they do not put on their résumé. However, you do not need to provide any personal details other than your contact information. For example, why include your date of birth? Age is not relevant for a position unless specifically stated. Likewise, omit your Social Security number, nationality, marital status, and a statement about health. Do not include a photograph with your CV unless one

TYPICAL INFORMATION CATEGORIES ON CVs

The following list presents the categories of information generally provided on the CVs of pharmacy professionals:

- Personal information

- Educational background

- Postgraduate training

- Professional practice experience

- Other work experience

- Licensure and certification

- Research experience

- Teaching experience

- Publications

- Presentations

- Professional memberships

- Service activities

- Awards and honors

- References

has been requested for a specific purpose. If asked to supply a photograph, use a passport-sized head shot.

Career Objective

As a general rule, most pharmacists and health professionals do not put a career objective on their curriculum vitae. You may want to include one, however, depending on how you intend to use the CV. For example, prospective employers who request your CV may appreciate seeing a career objective to get a sense of the type of position you're seeking. Sometimes, including a career objective can help highlight special knowledge and skills that you want to call to your reader's immediate attention.

Educational Experience

List your educational experience in reverse chronological order and include the name and location of the institution, dates attended, and the type of degree earned. If you took only one or two courses at an institution to fulfill a degree requirement, you do not need to include them. Also, you should not include high school credentials if you have a college degree or have earned at least two years of college credits.

You can present your academic standing as a cumulative grade point average, class ranking, or graduation honor (e.g., graduated magna cum laude). Most people consider it optional to include academic standing, but if you earned exceptional grades, you may want to highlight them. If you apply for a residency, fellowship, or graduate position, you should always include your academic standing.

Professional Training

If you have completed a residency or fellowship, earned certification as a technician, or received other professional training, you can list it in the education section, include it in the professional experience section, or create a separate section. It's your choice. If you consider your professional training an important extension of the educational process, for example, you may want to combine it with your educational background.

On the other hand, you may want to give it a separate heading if you don't want to overshadow your academic credentials and would like to call special attention to your internship or residency. Or, you may decide it fits best within the professional practice experience section, especially if the training was recent. In this case, it will stand out by falling at the top of your reverse chronological listing.

When listing professional training, make sure to include the name and location of the institution where you received your specialized training, dates attended, and the type of certificate or credential earned.

Professional Experience

The professional experience section deserves prominence on the curriculum vitae. Ideally, you should devote this section to your experience within the profession. Do not include other, less relevant work. Instead, include it elsewhere on your CV.

People at the beginning of their careers, however, may want to combine professional and other work experiences under a single heading such as "employment experience." Those with extensive professional experience may wish to leave out other work experience altogether, unless their history involves more than one established career.

You can include volunteer experience in this section if your commitment was sustained over time and required you to apply professional knowledge and skills. The experience gained through volunteerism, especially in a health care related activity, provides as much value as that acquired through a paid position. You can also consider placing this type of information in a section devoted to "public service," "community service," or "service activities."

When preparing your "professional experience" listings, include the following:

- Name and location of the employer or volunteer agency.

- Beginning and ending dates of employment.

- Title of the position held.

- A description of duties.

When describing each position, use action verbs to emphasize your accomplishments. Table 2.1 on pages 8-9 lists many common action verbs used in pharmacy-related résumés and CVs. Keep descriptions brief and organize key information using bullets or dashes. You don't need to give the supervisor's name and contact information for each position, especially if you have included one or more of these names in your reference list.

Licensure and Certification

Document the types of licenses and certificates you hold, as well as their status. Include the awarding agency, license number, date of issue, and most recent renewal date.

List certificates acknowledging the successful completion of training programs chronologically, with the most recent certificate first. State the full title of the certificate, the organization awarding it, and the date of certification. Examples of applicable certificates include a pharmacy technician training program, a residency training program, a cardiopulmonary resuscitation training program, or a Board of Pharmaceutical Specialties examination.

Research Experience

In this section, you can showcase all research and scholarly pursuits, including grants, contracts, patents, and projects. List them in reverse chronological order and include the title, sponsoring agency or corporation, funding requested, date of submission, and outcome of the submission. In general, these listings should not include a description of the work.

If you're a student, include the title of your research or scholarly activity, name of the institution, names of co-investigators such as a major professor or other faculty, and dates of the activity. You can also briefly describe the special knowledge or skills you acquired.

Teaching Experience

Many health professionals include teaching experience and faculty appointments on their CVs. Although you can place this information in the professional experience section, it achieves greater prominence if you create a special section. For each appointment or activity, list the institution, course number and title, date provided, and the number of students involved. Examples of teaching experience you can list on your CV include:

- Lecturing.

- Coordinating conferences.

- Giving workshops or recitation sessions.

- Serving as a mentor.

- Precepting students in a practice environment.

- Providing continuing education to practitioners.

- Preparing electronic course materials.

Publications

Publications you can list on your CV include articles you've published in professional journals, books you've authored, and reports you've prepared. You can also include scholarly work in nontraditional media such as electronic software packages or audiovisual productions.

For guidelines on how to cite publications properly, check standard reference guides such as *The Chicago Manual of Style* or the *American Medical Association Manual of Style*. Following a uniform style ensures that the order of each element (author, name of publication, date), as well as the way you use punctuation, italics, and other features, stays consistent for each publication you list.

Presentations

Presentations, especially invited presentations, reflect your professional experience and scholarship. They show prospective employers that you are knowledgeable, articulate, and a respected person in your field. List your presentations in reverse chronological order and provide the title of each, as well as the inviting or sponsoring organization, location, and date.

Awards and Honors

Whether you decide to announce your awards, honors, and other recognition near the beginning or end of your CV remains your preference. Because not everyone reads a CV through to the end, you may want to highlight a particularly impressive honor near the beginning. On the other hand, positioning a lengthy list of accolades near the end of the CV leaves room at the beginning for other key material. Use your judgment, but wherever you place awards and honors, use reverse chronological order. Include the name of the award, sponsoring organization, location where given, and date.

> **TIP:** If you participate extensively in professional organizations, consider creating a separate section on your CV entitled "leadership experience." This allows you to highlight specific offices you've held in various organizations and to elaborate a bit on your leadership role.

Professional Memberships

You can document membership in professional organizations or associations in a section entitled "professional memberships" or "membership in organizations." Provide the name of the organization and dates of membership (represented as "1994-Present" or "1994-2005"). In this section you can also highlight offices you've held or note other kinds of participation, such as committee memberships or task force assignments.

Service Activities

A section on service activities can document professional or personal efforts to meet the needs of the profession or community. Service to the profession, for example, might involve holding an office in an organization or serving on a university committee. Your listing of activities will reflect your own definition of service.

Make sure that you don't include items more than once in the CV's body. For example, if you list your volunteer activities in the professional experience section, do not repeat them in the service activities section.

References

The final item on your CV relates to references. As with résumés, do not list references on the curriculum vitae. Create a separate page that provides the name of each reference along with complete contact information, including mailing address, telephone number, fax number, and e-mail address. If desired, you can also include a brief statement about what each reference can contribute concerning your knowledge, skills, and abilities. Although some people send their reference page along with their CV, hold off until a prospective employer specifically requests your reference list.

Other Sections

Depending on your individual experience and attributes, you may want to include other sections. "Military service," for example, would note your branch of service, entry and discharge dates, rank, type of discharge, and reserves activity. Military service usually gets listed in reverse chronological order according to rank.

Your CV's Look

Just like résumés, CVs should be neat, appeal to the reader's eye, and adhere to basic guidelines for readability. Chapter 2 outlines these guidelines. If potential employers find your CV difficult to read, they may not bother. Also, proofread your CV carefully for typographical and mechanical errors. Make sure that each page carries your full name as well as a page number, in case pieces of the CV become separated.

Once you've developed a standard version of your curriculum vitae, consider preparing versions suitable for scanning and electronic transmission. Chapter 2 provides guidelines for creating scannable and electronic documents.

Chapter 5

Tips, Checklists, and Sample Curricula Vitae

TIP: Put your highest priority categories toward the beginning of your CV so readers see them easily.

In this chapter you'll find samples of curricula vitae (CV) with various headings, formats, and content. These samples present elements for you to pick and choose from to create an individualized CV. Keep in mind that the guidelines provided in Chapter 2 for organizing and preparing a résumé apply equally to a CV. As you finalize your CV, refer to the box on page 47, Final Checklist of CV Elements, to ensure you have not overlooked anything.

Design Tips

Just as with résumés, good readability and a clean appearance are crucial to successful CVs. The box to the right lists specific CV design tips.

Checklists

In Chapter 2, you'll find helpful suggestions for designing your CV in the section entitled "Your Résumé's Look." The box "Checklist for Preparing a CV" on page 46 contains a few other points to remember.

Electronic Formats

The content of your curriculum vitae will probably remain the same whether you prepare a standard, scannable, or electronic document. When preparing the latter two types, however, you may want to include specific keywords in case the employer uses computer software to search your CV electronically. Table 2.3 on page 13 lists common keywords for pharmacy-related electronic résumés and CVs.

Final Evaluation

After you've prepared your CV in what you consider final form, put it aside for a few days so you can look at it again with fresh eyes. Then go through it carefully one more time. Make sure you check:

- Accuracy of details. Are all your dates, titles, and other facts correct?

- Redundancy. Have you repeated the same information in more than one place?

As a final "quality control" measure, ask peers and mentors to critique your curriculum vitae. Also, check your CV against the final checklist on page 47.

DESIGN TIPS FOR CVS

- Because CVs contain so many category headings, make them stand out by using boldface, capitalized letters, italics, or underlining.

- Choose a consistent serif font (e.g., Bookman Old Style, Courier, Georgia, Times New Roman) or a sans serif font (e.g., Arial, Lucida Sans, Tahoma, Verdana).

- Use a font size between 10 and 14 points.

- Use various design formats (e.g., bullets, lines, italics, boldface type, shading) to create a unique appearance, but do not overuse them.

- Maintain one-inch margins at the top, bottom, and sides of the document.

- Justify the left margin.

- Avoid using graphics.

CHECKLIST FOR ELECTRONIC AND SCANNABLE CVs

The section entitled "Electronic Formats" in Chapter 2 (page 14) talks about preparing a résumé for transmission over the Internet and storage in computer databases. The same information applies to CVs. Here's a summary of the most important points:

- Choose a consistent sans serif font such as Arial, Lucida Sans, Tahoma, or Verdana. Keep your font size between 12 and 14 points.

- Minimize the use of design elements (e.g., bullets, lines, underlining, italics, boldface type, brackets, parentheses, shading).

- Avoid the use of tabs. Instead, create spaces using the spacebar.

- Use hard carriage returns at the end of each line.

- Do not use word wrapping.

- Include common keywords related to skills likely to be included in a computer search strategy.

- Check for spelling errors before saving as a text file.

- Use capital letters for headings as a replacement for boldface type or underlining.

- Maintain one-inch margins at the top, bottom, and sides of the document.

- Justify the left margin.

- For a scannable CV, save the final document as a "text only" or "rich text format" file. Once you have printed it on paper, do not fold or staple it.

- For an electronically transmitted CV, save the final document in a suitable format (e.g., HTML for web posting, ASCII or PDF for attaching to e-mail).

CHECKLIST FOR PREPARING A CV

- Use the present tense for current duties and activities, and the past tense for others.

- Write out numbers between one and nine and use numerals for 10 and above.

- Use a consistent format for telephone numbers and dates.

- Use the proper two-letter abbreviations for states.

- Achieve a reasonable balance between typed copy and white space so the material does not look overcrowded.

- Proofread your document carefully for grammar, spelling, syntax, and punctuation errors, and don't forget to use your computer's "spell check" feature.

- Use only one side of each page for printing.

Curricula Vitae Samples

On pages 48-76 you'll find examples of CVs for pharmacy professionals. The approaches vary and none of these examples is perfect for everyone. Review the formats, consider the comments on each one, and develop a CV that works for your needs.

FINAL CHECKLIST OF CV ELEMENTS

☐ HEADING
- The words "Curriculum Vitae" usually suffice.
- Full legal name or first name, middle initial, and last name.

☐ CONTACT INFORMATION
- Current address, telephone number (day and evening), and e-mail address.
- Permanent address, telephone number, and e-mail address (if applicable).

☐ DATE THE CV WAS PREPARED

☐ CAREER OBJECTIVE (OPTIONAL)
- Don't make your objective too vague or too specific. Make sure the objective coincides with any specific position you apply for.

☐ EDUCATION
- Name of each institution and location (i.e., city and state).
- Degree or degrees earned and year.
- List residency or fellowship training with year and name of institution and location, if not included as professional experience or under a separate heading.

☐ EXPERIENCE
- List positions in reverse chronological order.
- Include accurate position titles.
- List position responsibilities.
- Describe skills using action-oriented phrases.
- Quantify your accomplishments when applicable.

☐ LICENSES AND CERTIFICATES
- Consider listing licenses and certificates with dates, if not listed in the professional experience section.

☐ RESEARCH EXPERIENCE
- List grants, contracts, patents, and projects in reverse chronological order with the title, sponsoring agency or corporation, funding requested, date of submission, and outcome of the submission.
- For students, list the title of the research or scholarly activity, name of the institution, names of co-investigators such as a major professor or other faculty, and the dates of the activity.
- For students, consider including a brief description of special knowledge or skills acquired with any research or scholarly activity.

☐ TEACHING EXPERIENCE
- In reverse chronological order, list the type of teaching, such as lecturing, or coordinating conference, workshop, or recitation sessions; serving as a mentor; precepting students in a practice environment; providing continuing education to practitioners; or preparing electronic course materials. Start with the name of the institution, followed by course number and title, date provided, and the number of students involved.

☐ PUBLICATIONS
- List all articles, monographs, books, and other publications in reverse chronological order according to the format established for biomedical journals. For guidelines, check style guides such as *The Chicago Manual of Style* or the *American Medical Association Manual of Style*.
- List nontraditional publications such as electronic software packages or audio-visual productions according to the format established for biomedical journals.

☐ PRESENTATIONS
- List the title, inviting or sponsoring organization, location, and date of each presentation in reverse chronological order.

☐ AWARDS, HONORS, AND RECOGNITION
- Identify the title, sponsor, and date of significant recognition or awards.

☐ PROFESSIONAL MEMBERSHIPS
- List the organization and inclusive dates of membership.
- List any offices held or other evidence of participation.
- If you have an extensive list of memberships, consider a separate heading such as "leadership experience" to document achievements.

☐ SERVICE ACTIVITIES
- List activity, organization, city, state, and dates.
- Consider organizing entries by categories of service (e.g., profession, university, patient, community).

☐ REFERENCES
- Prepare a separate page and provide the name of each reference along with complete contact information including address, telephone number, fax number, and e-mail address.
- Consider preparing a brief statement about what each reference can contribute concerning your knowledge, skills, and abilities.

A clean, straightforward, "no-frills" CV for a health-system pharmacist who completed a one-year residency and has three years of experience in his current position. Font: Times New Roman 12 point.

Curriculum Vitae

Ryan David Freeman

Boise VA Medical Center
100 Medical Center Drive
Boise, Idaho 83706
Telephone: (208) 757-0935
Fax: (208) 659-1840
E-mail: ryan.freeman@.boiseva.gov

2501 Nickerson Court
Boise, Idaho 83702
Telephone: (208) 225-8562
E-mail: rdfree@greatnet.com

OBJECTIVE

To obtain a pharmacist supervisor position in a health-system pharmacy.

EDUCATION

Idaho State University
College of Pharmacy
Pocatello, Idaho

Doctor of Pharmacy degree
August 1998 – May 2002

University of Nevada at Reno
Reno, Nevada

Pre-Pharmacy Curriculum
September 1995 – June 1998

EXPERIENCE

Boise VA Medical Center
Boise, Idaho

Clinical Pharmacist
August 2003 – Present

Veterans Affairs Medical Center
8740 South Harbor Boulevard
Harbor City, California

Primary Care Pharmacy
Practice Residency
July 2002 – June 2003

St. Mary's Hospital
Reno, Nevada

Pharmacy Intern
Summers, 1999 and 2000

Walgreen's Pharmacy
Reno, Nevada

Pharmacy Technician
July 1996 – July 1998
Part-time

Nevada Seismological Laboratory
University of Nevada at Reno
Reno, Nevada

Transcription Technician
October 1995 – June 1996
Part-time

Actual CV size is 8.5 x 11

Ryan David Freeman
Curriculum Vitae, Page 2

PHARMACY PRACTICE EXPERIENCE ROTATIONS

Primary Care Pharmacy Residency
Veterans Affairs Medical Center, Harbor City, California

- Required Rotation – 9 months

    Ambulatory Care Clinic
    Preceptor: Michael Ko, Pharm.D.

- Elective Rotations – 2 months total

    Santa Ana Family Medicine Center
    Santa Ana, California
    Preceptor: Jeannette Livingston, Pharm.D.

    Jackson Healthcare Nursing Home
    Fullerton, California
    Preceptor: Marian Baker, Pharm.D.

- Concurrent Rotations – 4 hours per week for 10 months

    Anticoagulation Clinic
    Preceptor: Michael Ko, Pharm.D.

    Infectious Diseases Clinic
    Preceptor: Kristin Barnes, Pharm.D.

Doctor of Pharmacy Degree Program
Idaho State University, Pocatello, Idaho

- Required Rotations – 7 months total

    Hospital Pharmacy Practice
    Moreno Valley Community Hospital, Moreno Valley, California
    Preceptor: Lisa Moore, M.S., R.Ph.

    Internal Medicine
    Irvine Medical Center, Irvine, California
    Preceptor: Tracey Chan, Pharm.D.

Ryan David Freeman
Curriculum Vitae, Page 3

- Required Rotations – 7 months total (Continued)

  Community Pharmacy Practice
  Albertson's Pharmacy, Irvine, California
  Preceptor: Kamy Lee, Pharm.D.

  Primary Care
  Kaiser Permanente Hospital, San Diego, California
  Preceptor: Jason Neu, Pharm.D.

  Psychiatry
  Pocatello Regional Medical Center, Pocatello, Idaho
  Preceptor: Thao Nguyen, Pharm.D.

  Drug Information
  Pocatello Regional Medical Center, Pocatello, Idaho
  Preceptor: Harold Weiss, Pharm.D.

- Elective Rotations – 2 months total

  Infectious Diseases
  Pocatello Regional Medical Center, Pocatello, Idaho
  Preceptor: Courtney Scott, Pharm.D.

  Administration
  Idaho Board of Pharmacy, Pocatello, Idaho
  Preceptor: Frederick Hamilton, R.Ph.

LICENSES

Idaho State Board of Pharmacy – 2002   Pharmacist No. 1138, examination

California State Board of Pharmacy – 2002   Pharmacist No. 013772, examination

Nevada Board of Pharmacy – 2003   Pharmacist No. 4961, reciprocity

Ryan David Freeman
Curriculum Vitae, Page 4

PUBLICATIONS

Freeman RD, Ko MA, Young HF. An analysis of pharmaceutical care outcome measures in patients receiving antiretroviral drug therapy. *Am J Health-Syst Pharm*. In Press.

Freeman RD. The Pharmacist's Role in Wellness and Disease Prevention. *Idaho Pharmacist*. 2005; 49:24-27.

SELECTED PRESENTATIONS

June 2005	"The Pharmacist's Role in Wellness and Disease Prevention" presented to members of the Idaho Pharmaceutical Association, Pocatello, Idaho.
October 2004	"Perspectives on Immunization Therapy" presented at Medical Grand Rounds, Boise VA Medical Center, Boise, Idaho.
December 2003	"The Evaluation of Pharmaceutical Care Outcome Measures in Patients Receiving Antiretroviral Drug Therapy" presented as a poster at the American Society of Health-System Pharmacists Midyear Clinical Meeting, Atlanta, Georgia.
October 2003	"Minimizing the Adverse Effects of Oral Anticoagulation Therapy" presented at Medical Grand Rounds, Veterans Affairs Medical Center, Harbor City, California.
May 2003	"An evaluation of the Pharmacoeconomic Impact of Pharmacist Interventions in an Infectious Diseases Clinic" presented at the Western Pharmacy Residency Conference, Anaheim, California.
April 2003	"Drug Management of Prostatitis" presented to Team II medical residents and interns at the Veterans Affairs Medical Center, Harbor City, California.
February 2003	"Novel Drug Therapies for the Management of HIV/AIDS Patients" presented to members of the Departments of Nursing and Pharmacy at the Veterans Affairs Medical Center, Harbor City, California.
December 2002	"Application of Knowledge in a Primary Care Pharmacy Practice Residency" presented to students and faculty at the University of Idaho College of Pharmacy, Pocatello, Idaho.

Ryan David Freeman
Curriculum Vitae, Page 5

PROFESSIONAL MEMBERSHIPS

American Society of Health-System Pharmacists	2002 – Present
California Society of Health-System Pharmacists	2002 – 1998
Idaho Pharmacists Association	1998 – Present
American Pharmacists Association	1998 – Present

LEADERSHIP EXPERIENCE

Idaho Pharmacists Association

• Treasurer	2004 – 2005
• Chairman, Membership Committee	2003 – 2004

Idaho State University, School of Pharmacy

• Phi Delta Chi, President	2001 – 2002
• Phi Lambda Sigma, Treasurer	2000 – 2001
• Academy of Students of Pharmacy, Vice President	2000 – 2001

SERVICE ACTIVITIES

American Cancer Society, Boise Idaho

• Coordinator, Great American Smoke-Out Event	2004

American Red Cross Blood Drive, Harbor City, California

• Team Captain, VA Medical Center	March, 2003

Boy Scouts of America, Reno, Nevada

• Leader, Troop 12	1996

AWARDS AND RECOGNITION

Veterans Affairs Medical Center, Harbor City, California

• Outstanding Resident Award	2003

Idaho State University, Pocatello, Idaho

• Outstanding Pharmacy Leader Award	2002
• J. Alan Simpson Scholarship	2001

REFERENCES

Available upon request

A CV for a community pharmacist in practice 12 years who also has hospital and teaching experience. Font: Lucida Sans 12 point.

CURRICULUM VITAE

Ellen Lee Woodruff

942 Derbyshire Court
Tallahassee, Florida 32302
(850) 564-7820
elwood@advancelink.com

> *List of responsibilities is clear and concise; she could consider emphasizing and quantifying achievements in each position, such as "administer [number] immunizations per year" or "compound [number] medications annually."*

QUALIFICATIONS PROFILE

Pharmacist with eight years of community pharmacy practice and four years of hospital pharmacy practice. Taught high school chemistry for three years. Dedicated to community service activities.

PHARMACY PRACTICE EXPERIENCE

Jay's Apothecary   2002 – Present
1210 South Point Boulevard
Tallahasee, Florida 32306
(850) 721-8000
Supervisor: Jay T. Roberts, Pharm.D.

Responsibilities: Participate in disease state management services for patients with asthma, diabetes and lipid disorders; administer immunizations; evaluate and dispense prescriptions for patients; counsel patients on the proper use of their medications and related devices; compound extemporaneous prescription products; and precept pharmacy students and interns.

Coastal Pharmacy   1999 – 2001
859 Coastal Avenue
Oceanside, California 92052
(760) 345-9000
Supervisor: Bao H. Nguyen, Pharm.D.

> *Including supervisors' names is optional but not necessary, especially for someone with several years of practice experience. These could appear in a separate list of references.*

Ellen Lee Woodruff
Curriculum Vitae
Page 2

PHARMACY PRACTICE EXPERIENCE (Continued)

Responsibilities: Compounded prescriptions in specific dosage forms for human and veterinary use; demonstrated proper use of compounding equipment to pharmacy personnel; promoted availability of compounding services to physicians and other health care professionals in the community; evaluated and dispensed prescriptions for patients; counseled patients on proper use of their medications and related devices; and assisted in precepting pharmacy interns.

Rite Aid Pharmacy   1998 – 1999
1800 Vista Way
Oceanside, California 92056
(760) 722-2040
Pharmacist in Charge: Elaine Magee, R.Ph.

Responsibilities: Received and interpreted written prescriptions from prescribers; determined health plan eligibility for patients; dispensed medications; maintained computer records of prescriptions dispensed; maintained a health information display center containing printed health information materials for the public; and counseled patients on proper use of their medications and related devices.

Walgreens Pharmacy   1997 – 1998
10875 Poway Highway
Poway, California 92074
(858) 745-6700
Pharmacist in Charge: Alice Chen, R.Ph.

Responsibilities: Received and interpreted written prescriptions from prescribers; determined health plan eligibility for patients; dispensed medication; maintained computer records of prescriptions dispensed; maintained an inventory of prescription and nonprescription drug products; and counseled patients on proper use of their medications and related devices.

Tacoma General Hospital   1993 – 1997
304 Madison Street
Tacoma, Washington 98356
(253) 812-3872
Pharmacist in Charge: Liang Yuen, Pharm.D.

Ellen Lee Woodruff
Curriculum Vitae
Page 3

PHARMACY PRACTICE EXPERIENCE (Continued)

Responsibilities: Received and interpreted written prescriptions for hospitalized patients; reviewed prescription orders for potential drug interactions, allergies, and adverse events; reviewed prescription orders for formulary status and recommended therapeutic alternatives when appropriate; assured accuracy of medication orders completed by pharmacy technicians; provided drug information services to physicians and nurses; prepared and dispensed small- and large-volume parenteral intravenous solutions; maintained an inventory of controlled substances and investigational drugs; provided medication counseling to patients at the time of their hospital discharge; and, assisted in preparing a monthly departmental newsletter.

PROFESSIONAL DEVELOPMENT

Professional Compounding Centers of America Continuing Education Program	2000 and 2003
Health Supports and Appliances Certification Program National Community Pharmacists Association	2002

EDUCATION

St. John's University, Jamaica, New York College of Pharmacy and Allied Health Programs Bachelor of Science in Pharmacy	1989 – 1992
Onondaga Community College, Syracuse, New York Pre-Pharmacy Course Work Completed	1988 – 1989
Syracuse University School of Education and College of Arts and Sciences Syracuse, New York Bachelor of Science in Chemistry	1977 – 1981

Ellen Lee Woodruff
Curriculum Vitae
Page 4

LICENSES AND CERTIFICATES

Florida Board of Pharmacy (#12678, by examination)	2002
California State Board of Pharmacy (# 41689, by examination)	1997
Washington State Board of Pharmacy (# R-09737, by reciprocity)	1993
New York Board of Pharmacy (#19-027305, by examination)	1992
New York State Teaching Certificate	1981

TEACHING EXPERIENCE

Clinical Assistant Professor   2004 – Present
University of Florida, Gainesville, Florida

Clinical Assistant Professor   2004 – Present
Florida A and M University, Tallahassee, Florida

Practitioner-Teacher   2000 – 2001
University of Southern California, Los Angeles,

Chemistry Teacher   1981 – 1984
West Syracuse High School, Syracuse, New York

PRESENTATIONS

"Osteoporosis and You" presented to members of the Tallahassee Women's Club, Tallahassee, Florida, October 2002.

"Ostomy and Incontinence Care" presented to Oceanside Ostomy Support Group, Oceanside, California, April 2000.

"Safety Rules for Your Medicine Cabinet" presented as an interview with WTCW-TV, Tacoma, Washington, February, 1995.

"Smoking and Your Health" presented to members of the National Honor Society, Foxworth High School, Tacoma, Washington, October 1994.

"Tips for Medication Childproofing Your Home" presented to members of the Powell Middle School Parent-Teachers Association, Tacoma, Washington, March 1994.

Ellen Lee Woodruff
Curriculum Vitae
Page 5

PROFESSIONAL AND COMMUNITY AFFILIATIONS

Florida Pharmacists Association	2002 – Present
Tallahassee Women's Club	2002 – Present
National Community Pharmacists Association	2001 – Present
Washington Pharmacists Association	1994 – 1997

- Member, Public Affairs Committee, 1996

American Institute of the History of Pharmacy	1994 – Present
Powell Middle School Parent-Teacher's Association	1993 – 1997
Tacoma, Washington	

- Vice-President, 1995 – 1996
- President, 1996 – 1997

Tacoma Women's Club	1993 – 1997
American Pharmacists Association	1990 – Present

AWARDS AND RECOGNITION

American Cancer Society Award for smoking cessation activities in the community, California	1999
Most Outstanding Member Award Tacoma Women's Club	1997

REFERENCES

Provided Upon Request

A concise, easy-to-read CV for a recent pharmacy graduate interested in academia.
Font: Times New Roman 11 and 12 point.

Mylinh Le Pham

Curriculum Vitae

> *A summary statement at the beginning is optional but would be useful for highlighting this pharmacist's strengths, such as public speaking experience.*

PERSONAL

Current Address

305 Parkland Road
Richmond, Virginia 23235
804.781.8873
mlpham3@vcu.edu

Permanent Address

9149 Mill Court Drive
Alexandria, Virginia 22314
703.549.2386
mylinh.pham@earthnet.com

OBJECTIVE

To gain a non-tenure faculty position in pharmacy practice

EDUCATION

2000 – 2004

Virginia Commonwealth University
Medical College of Virginia Campus
School of Pharmacy
Richmond, Virginia
Doctor of Pharmacy degree
Conferred: May 2004

1996 – 2000

Virginia Polytechnic Institute and State
University, Blacksburg, Virginia
B.S. in Biochemistry degree
Conferred: May 2000

SPECIALIZED TRAINING

2004 – 2005

> *To highlight her unique skills she could add a couple of bullet points with a bit more detail and some accomplishments in the sections on training, professional experience, research, and teaching.*

Community Pharmacy Practice Residency
Virginia Commonwealth University
School of Pharmacy
Richmond, Virginia
Program Director: John Harmon, Pharm.D.
Certificate Awarded: May 2005

Actual CV size is 8.5 x 11

Mylinh Le Pham
Curriculum Vitae
Page 2

PROFESSIONAL EXPERIENCE

Pharmacy Practice Clerkships
(May 2003 – May 2004)

Acute Care – Adult Medicine
Medical College of Virginia Hospitals, Richmond, VA
Preceptor: Barbara Muncy, Pharm.D.

Primary Ambulatory Care
Veteran's Administration Hospital, Richmond, VA
Preceptor: William Morris, Pharm.D.

Health-Systems Practice
St. Mary's Hospital, Richmond, VA
Preceptor: Francis Myles, Pharm.D.

Community Practice
Lynchburg Apothecary, Lynchburg, VA
Preceptor: Lee Philips, R.Ph.

Long Term Care
Ridgeview Nursing Center, Roanoke, VA
Preceptor: Mary Tucker, R.Ph.

Elective – Primary Ambulatory Care
PHS Indian Health Center, Fort Duchesne, UT
Preceptor: Howard Stewart, Pharm.D.

Elective – Association Management
Virginia Pharmacists Association, Richmond, VA
Preceptor: Betty Schumaker, R.Ph.

Elective – Psychiatry
Medical College of Virginia Hospitals, Richmond, VA
Preceptor: Tim Bolton, Pharm.D.

Internship
(Summers 2001 & 2002)

Pharmacy Intern
Tidwell Pharmacy, Alexandria, VA
Preceptor: Julia Tidwell, R.Ph.

Employment
(Summers 1999 & 2000)

Pharmacy Technician
Alexandria Hospital, Alexandria, VA
Preceptor: Hugh Chan

Mylinh Le Pham
Curriculum Vitae
Page 3

LICENSES AND CERTIFICATES

July 2004 – Present

Pharmacist, License No. 5862
Commonwealth of Virginia

April 2003 – Present

Advanced Cardiac Life Support Provider
American Heart Association

RESEARCH EXPERIENCE

September 2004 – Present

Assessing the outcome of nonprescription
medication use in a diabetic population

TEACHING EXPERIENCE

July 2004 – Present

Instructor in Pharmacy
Virginia Commonwealth University
- Lecturer, PHAR-742 (Pharmacotherapy III)
- Lecturer, PHAR-648 (Women's Health)
- Preceptor, PHAR-766 (Community Ambulatory
Care Practice)

PUBLICATIONS

2006

Pham ML, Toth HR. The consequences of nonprescription medication use in a diabetic population. *Am
J Health-Syst Pharm.* Submitted for publication

2004

Pham ML. New strategies in managing allergic rhinitis.
Virginia Pharmacist 2004; 88 (7): 24-26.

PRESENTATIONS

May 2005

"Managing nonprescription medication use for diabetic
patients" presented to members of the Old Dominion
Pharmaceutical Association, Lynchburg, Virginia

April 2005

"Advances in devices to administer medications to
asthmatics" presented to the nursing staff of the Visiting
Nurses Association, Richmond, Virginia

Mylinh Le Pham
Curriculum Vitae
Page 4

PRESENTATIONS (Continued)

April 2005	"Dealing with drug formulary decision making" presented to physicians and staff of the Virginia Medical Associates, Fredericksburg, Virginia
February 2005	"The treatment of hyperlipidemia with lovastatin" presented to members of the Tidewater Pharmacists Association, Chesapeake, Virginia
January 2005	"Community Pharmacy Residency Programs" presented to members of the Class of 2006, VCU School of Pharmacy, Richmond, Virginia
November 2004	"The benefits of a pharmacy-based immunization program" presented to patients of the Buxton Place Pharmacy, Petersburg, Virginia
October 2004	"The use of low molecular weight heparin for ambulatory patients" presented to the pharmacy staff of St. John's Hospital, Johnson City, Virginia
August 2004	"Advances in treating asthma" presented to members of the Richmond Asthma Support Group, Richmond, Virginia
March 2004	"The treatment of gout and hyperuricemia" presented to students and faculty of the VCU School of Pharmacy, Richmond, Virginia

PROFESSIONAL MEMBERSHIPS

2003 – Present	Rho Chi Pharmaceutical Honor Society
2002 – 2004	Student Chapter, National Community Pharmacists Association
2002 – 2004	Student National Pharmaceutical Association
2001 – Present	Kappa Epsilon Professional Pharmacy Fraternity
2000 – Present	American Pharmacists Association
2000 – Present	Virginia Pharmacists Association
2000 – Present	American Society of Health-System Pharmacists
2000 – 2004	Virginia Academy of Students of Pharmacy

Mylinh Le Pham
Curriculum Vitae
Page 5

LEADERSHIP EXPERIENCE

2004 – 2005	Virginia Pharmacists Association • Member, Policy Committee
2003 – 2004	Kappa Epsilon Professional Pharmacy Fraternity • Vice-President
2002 – 2004	Virginia Academy of Students of Pharmacy • President, 2003 – 2004 • Secretary, 2002 – 2003 • Alternate Delegate, 2002

COMMUNITY SERVICE

April 2005	Alzheimer's Association Memory Walk
March 2005	Richmond Pharmacists Association Health Fair
January 2005	Pharmacy Day 2000 at the Virginia Legislature
October 2004	Richmond Pharmacists Association Diabetes Screening Clinic
September 2004	WRVA Health Awareness Campaign
May 2004	American Cancer Society's Relay for Life
November 2003	Virginia Pharmacists Operation Immunization Project
September 2002	Poison Prevention Awareness Program at Chester Middle School, Chester, Virginia

AWARDS AND HONORS

2004	Pharmacy Communications Award
2004	American Pharmacists Association – Academy of Students of Pharmacy Mortar and Pestle Award
2003	Johnson Academic Scholarship
2001 – 2004	Dean's List of Outstanding Students (Fall and Spring semesters)

Mylinh Le Pham
Curriculum Vitae
Page 6

REFERENCES

> The list of references at the end is not customary, but you can add such a list if you choose.

John Harmon, Pharm.D.
Professor of Pharmacy
School of Pharmacy
Virginia Commonwealth University
410 North 12th Street
Richmond, Virginia 23298-0674
Telephone: (804) 828-4976
E-mail: jaharmon@vcu.edu

Judith R. Townsend, Pharm.D.
Assistant Professor of Pharmacy
School of Pharmacy
Virginia Commonwealth University
410 North 12th Street
Richmond, Virginia 23298-0674
Telephone: (804) 828-3129
E-mail: jrtownse@vcu.edu

Monica A. West, R.Ph.
Buxton Place Pharmacy
308 Buxton Place
Petersburg, Virginia 23803
Telephone: (804) 786-4000
E-mail: monica.west@snapnet.com

Frank C. Walker, M.D.
Associate Professor of Medicine
School of Medicine
Virginia Commonwealth University
1101 East Marshall Street
Richmond, Virginia 23298-0972
Telephone: (804) 828-0388
E-mail: fcwalker@vcu.edu

A CV for a student about to graduate who is looking for a hospital pharmacy residency.
Font: Lucida Bright 10, 11, and 12 point.

CURRICULUM VITAE

SAMANTHA CHRISTINE LEWIS

Local Residence
4990 Warren Street
Cincinnati, Ohio 45214
Phone: (513) 651-6022
E-Mail: sclewis@zipnet.com

Permanent Residence
4804 Lamar Boulevard
Dayton, Ohio 45406
Phone: (937) 277-9758

Quantifying key achievements, perhaps in a summary statement at the beginning, would give readers a snapshot of her strengths.

OBJECTIVE

To obtain a pharmacy practice residency in a health-system pharmacy.

EDUCATION

September 1999 – Present

University of Cincinnati, College of Pharmacy
Cincinnati, Ohio
Doctor of Pharmacy
Degree anticipated May 2005

Format allows readers to skim quickly.

PROFESSIONAL EXPERIENCE

Provides succinct descriptions of duties in each internship.

March 2001 – Present

Pharmacy Intern
Christ Hospital, Cincinnati, Ohio
Preceptor: Elaine Curtis, R.Ph.

Activities include dispensing inpatient unit dose medications, responding to drug information requests from nurses, and preparing intravenous admixtures, including parenteral nutrition solutions and chemotherapy.

July 1997 – March 2001

Pharmacy Technician
Good Samaritan Hospital, Cincinnati, Ohio
Supervisor: Harold Gibson, R.Ph.

Activities included filling inpatient medication orders, preparing intravenous admixtures, compounding, and inventory functions for controlled substances.

April 1994 – April 1995

Pharmacy Clerk
Krogers Pharmacy, Ft. Mitchell, Kentucky
Supervisor: Tricia Stevens

Activities included processing insurance claims, maintaining inventory, and cashier duties.

SAMANTHA CHRISTINE LEWIS

PHARMACY PRACTICE ROTATIONS

March 2005 – April 2005	Elective – Acute Care – Infectious Diseases University Hospital, Cincinnati, Ohio Preceptor: Elizabeth Crowder, Pharm.D.

Activities included daily rounds with Infectious Disease Consult Service, monitoring and assessing appropriateness of antibiotic therapy, taking patient medication histories, performing pharmacokinetics calculations for dosage recommendations of antibiotics, and patient counseling.

February 2005 – March 2005	Primary Ambulatory Care Browning's Pharmacy, Montgomery, Ohio Preceptor: Todd Edmonds, Pharm.D.

Activities included assisting in developing a smoking cessation program, monitoring drug therapy of patients with chronic diseases, responding to drug information requests from physicians and nurses, documenting patient interventions, and processing and dispensing prescriptions.

January 2005 – February 2005	Nursing Home Practice Schwartz Pharmacy, Cincinnati, Ohio Preceptor: Suzanna Ward, R.Ph.

Activities included administering immunizations, stocking automated dispensing devices, conducting monthly nursing home chart reviews, reviewing medication pass procedures with nurses, and attending quality assurance committee meetings.

November 2004 – December 2004	Community Practice Walgreens Pharmacy, Covington, Kentucky Preceptor: Terry Barker, R.Ph.

Activities included preparing and dispensing prescription medications, receiving verbal prescriptions from physicians, counseling patients about prescription medications, and assessing and recommending nonprescription medications.

PHARMACY PRACTICE ROTATIONS (Continued)

October 2004 – November 2004

Elective – General Surgery
University Hospital, Cincinnati, Ohio
Preceptor: Julie Wright, Pharm.D.

Activities included attending daily rounds with general surgery team, monitoring drug therapy, developing drug therapy treatment plans, and participating in a drug usage evaluation of vancomycin therapy.

September 2004 – October 2004

Acute Care – Oncology
University Hospital, Cincinnati, Ohio
Preceptor: Rebecca Reaves, Pharm.D.

Activities included monitoring and assessing the appropriateness of chemotherapy, assisting with record keeping for investigational chemotherapeutic agents, collecting data for a drug usage evaluation for ondansetron therapy, and attending multidisciplinary team meetings for the discharge planning of patients.

August 2004 – September 2004

Acute Care – Medicine
St. Luke Hospital – East, Ft. Thomas, Kentucky
Preceptor: William Crowder, Pharm.D.

Activities included attending daily rounds with physicians, taking patient medication histories, performing pharmacokinetics dosage calculations for selected drugs, responding to drug information requests from nurses and physicians, and detecting and reporting adverse drug reactions,

July 2004 – August 2004

Health-System Practice
Fort Hamilton Hospital, Hamilton, Ohio
Preceptor: Jason Friedman, R.Ph.

Activities included entering physician orders into computer system, filling inpatient medication orders, delivering unit-dose cassettes to patient care areas, preparing intravenous admixture solutions, conducting an in-service education program for nurses, conducting nursing unit inspections, and responding to drug information requests.

SAMANTHA CHRISTINE LEWIS

PHARMACY PRACTICE ROTATIONS (Continued)

June 2004 – July 2004

Acute Care – Medicine
University Hospital, Cincinnati, Ohio
Preceptor: Sarah Nichols, Pharm.D.

Activities included attending daily rounds with adult medicine team, monitoring drug therapy for assigned patients and making recommendations to preceptor and team, and collecting data for a drug usage evaluation.

CERTIFICATES and LICENSES

2004 – Present

Basic Life Support Provider
American Heart Association

2001 – Present

Pharmacy Intern License No. 4698
Ohio Board of Pharmacy

PROFESSIONAL MEMBERSHIPS

1999 – Present

University of Cincinnati
Academy of Students of Pharmacy

1999 – Present

American Pharmacists Association

1999 – Present

Ohio Pharmacists Association

1999 – Present

Kappa Epsilon
   • President, 2003 – 2004
   • Secretary, 2002 – 2003
   • Chaplain, 2001 – 2002

PRESENTATIONS

April 2005

"Reducing Occupational Exposure to Bloodborne Pathogens" presented to faculty and students, College of Pharmacy

October 2004

"Cyclosporine Therapy" presented to faculty and students, College of Pharmacy

July 2004

"Drug Management of Pregnancy-Induced Hypertension" presented to medical team and 3 West nursing staff, University Hospital

SAMANTHA CHRISTINE LEWIS   PAGE 5

COMMUNITY SERVICE

2005   Kappa Epsilon Easter Egg Hunt
                                           Simpson Elementary School, Hamilton, Ohio

2004   Project Angel Tree
                                           Salvation Army, Newport, Kentucky

2002 – 2003   Volunteer, Habitat for Humanity

Summer 1999   Counselor, Camp Juniper for Girls
                                           Madison, Ohio

AWARDS AND HONORS

2004   Finalist, Patient Counseling Competition
                                           U.C. Academy of Students of Pharmacy

2004 – Present   Member, Phi Lambda Sigma

2000   Elks Foundation Scholarship

REFERENCES

Available upon request

A readable, nicely designed CV for a pharmacist currently involved in a pharmacy practice fellowship.
Font: Century Schoolbook 10 and 12 point.

CURRICULUM VITAE

Marianna Alicia Garcia

Local Address	**Permanent Address**
3663 Madison Place	7320 Lakewood Drive
Chicago, Illinois 60619	Springfield, Illinois 62702
(773) 846-6092	(217) 522-5164
E-mail: garcia08@uic.edu	

Education

University of Illinois at Chicago College of Pharmacy Chicago, Illinois	Doctor of Pharmacy Degree awarded June 2002
University of Illinois at Springfield Springfield, Illinois	Pre-Pharmacy Curriculum September 1996 – June 1999

Specialized Training

Industrial Pharmacy Practice Fellowship	Hoffmann-LaRoche, Inc. Nutley, New Jersey and Rutgers University College of Pharmacy Piscataway, New Jersey Certificate expected June 2006
Specialized Residency in Drug Information Practice	University of Illinois at Chicago College of Pharmacy Chicago, Illinois Certificate awarded June 2004
Pharmacy Practice Residency	St. John's Hospital Chicago, Illinois Certificate awarded June 2003

Marianna Alicia Garcia   Page 2

Professional Experience

Industrial Pharmacy Practice Fellowship
2004 – 2006

Hoffman-LaRoche, Inc., Clinical
Pharmacology Department and
Rutgers University

Experience Gained:
- Protocol design
- Developing case report forms
- Selecting investigators and sites
- Preparing operating budgets
- Contract negotiations
- Monitoring study sites
- Reviewing drug supply management procedures
- Managing and analyzing data
- Preparing final study reports
- Developing professional product information
- Participating in research quality assurance

Here, the "Experience Gained" sections make proper use of action verbs in a concise listing.

Specialized Residency in Drug
Information Practice
2003 – 2004

University of Illinois at Chicago
College of Pharmacy

Experience Gained:
- Developed plans for establishing new drug information service and for documenting its impact
- Developed medication use policies and procedures
- Participated in drug information service quality assurance
- Prepared drug literature evaluations supporting formulary management, disease state management guidelines, and drug therapy guidelines
- Researched and edited newsletters for health professionals
- Monitored the reporting of medication errors and adverse drug reactions
- Conducted medication use evaluations
- Analyzed financial and clinical outcomes

Marianna Alicia Garcia

Page 3

Professional Experience (Continued)

Pharmacy Practice Residency
2003 – 2004

St. John's Hospital
Chicago, Illinois

Experience Gained:
- Adult internal medicine
- Pain service
- Drug information
- Hematology/oncology
- Infectious diseases
- Pediatrics
- Home infusion service
- Pharmacy administration
- Ambulatory patient care

Listings of rotations are fine, but some employers appreciate a bit more detail about what was unique or exceptional about the experience.

Doctor of Pharmacy Program
1999 – 2002

University of Illinois at Chicago
College of Pharmacy

Experience Gained:
- General medicine
- Psychiatry
- Administration
- Community Practice
- Ambulatory Care
- Hospital Practice
- Drug Information

Licensure and Certification

Board of Pharmaceutical Specialties

Pharmacotherapy Specialist,
2004 – Present

New Jersey Board of Pharmacy
Illinois Board of Pharmacy

Pharmacist, License No. 2187, 1998
Pharmacist, License No. 3378, 1997

Academic Appointments

Rutgers University
College of Pharmacy

Clinical Assistant Professor
2004 – Present

University of Illinois at Chicago
College of Pharmacy

Instructor in Pharmacy
2002 – 2004

Marianna Alicia Garcia   Page 4

Publications

Garcia MA, Williamson TN. Resolving Medicare reimbursement issues for the use of prodrugs. *Pharmacotherapy*. 2005; 25:251-257.

Garcia MA, Johnson CR, Freeman PK. Cost-effectiveness of capecitabine versus anthracycline-containing chemotherapy regimens in the treatment of metastatic breast cancer. *Pharmacotherapy*. 2004; 24:957-962.

Garcia MA, Sniderman HJ. The impact of pharmacoeconomic research on reimbursement policies. *Med Care*. 2004; 42:514-520.

Presentations at National Meetings

Garcia MA. *Reimbursement strategies for the use of prodrugs*. Paper presented at Washington: Annual Meeting of the American Pharmacists Association; March 2005.

Garcia MA. *Drug therapy options for patients with metastatic breast cancer*. Poster presented at Kansas City: Annual Meeting of the American College of Clinical Pharmacy; July 2004.

Current Professional Affiliations

American College of Clinical Pharmacy
American Pharmacists Association
Drug Information Association
American Society of Health-System Pharmacists

Awards and Recognition

Chief Pharmacy Resident, University of Illinois College of Pharmacy, 2003 – 2004
Phi Kappa Phi, University of Illinois, 2002
Patient Care Award, University of Illinois College of Pharmacy, 2002
Leon J. Schwartz Scholarship, University of Illinois College of Pharmacy, 2001
Rho Chi Honor Society, Phi Chapter, University of Illinois, 2000

References

Provided upon request

Condensed version of an academic CV for a tenured professor shows a useful way of listing grants, publications, and presentations. Font: Verdana 11 and 10 point.

> Note: This is a condensed version of a 47-page curriculum vitae

Curriculum Vitae
2005

> *Because CVs are updated many times over the course of your career, including the year affirms for readers that this is the most current version.*

Glenn Michael Richards

PERSONAL INFORMATION

Home Address:

4350 Old Lexington Road
Athens, GA 30608
Telephone: 706-469-6683
E-mail: glenn.ricards@earthlink.com

Office Address:

College of Pharmacy
The University of Georgia
Athens, Georgia 30602
Telephone: (706) 542-5278
Telefax: (706) 542-7652
E-mail: gmrichar@rx.uga.edu

EDUCATION

1974 – 1978

Doctor of Philosophy, Medicinal Chemistry
State University of New York, School of Pharmacy, Buffalo, New York

1972 – 1974

Master of Science, Medicinal Chemistry
Northeastern University, College of Pharmacy, Boston, Massachusetts

1967 – 1972

Bachelor of Science, Pharmacy
Northeastern University, College of Pharmacy, Boston, Massachusetts

POSTDOCTORAL EXPERIENCE

1978 – 1980

Alcohol, Drug Abuse, Mental Health Administration Postdoctoral Fellow in Psychopharmacology, Department of Pharmacology and Experimental Therapeutics, State University of New York, School of Medicine, Buffalo, New York

Actual CV size is 8.5 x 11

Glenn Michael Richards
Curriculum vitae
Page 2

PROFESSIONAL POSITIONS

Department of Medicinal Chemistry, School of Pharmacy, University of Georgia
- 2003 – Present   Vice-Chair
- 1988 – Present   Professor with Tenure
- 1985 – 1988   Associate Professor with Tenure
- 1980 – 1985   Assistant Professor

Department of Pharmacology and Toxicology, School of Medicine, University of Georgia
- 1991 – Present   Affiliate Professor

Bon Secours Hospital, Boston, Massachusetts
- 1973 – 1974   Staff Pharmacist (Part-time)

Warner-Lambert Research Institute, Morris Plains, New Jersey
- 1972 – 1973   Research Chemist

HONORS

American Association of Colleges of Pharmacy
- Volwiler Research Achievement Award, 2004

American Pharmacists Association
- Research Achievement Award, 2001

University of Georgia
- Distinguished Scholar Award, 1998

University of Georgia, School of Pharmacy
- Professor of the Year Award, 1984 and 1989

RESEARCH EXPERIENCE (2005)

Grants (approved and funded)
- Chemical/behavioral studies on hallucinogenic agents, National Institutes of Health, $459,840.
- Development of novel serotonin agonists, Alza Laboratories, $112,755.
- Designing mechanism-based agonists for selected hallucinogens, National Science Foundation, $88,227.

Patents
- Richards GM, Snider TA, Johnson FB. Signal serotonin modifier compounds, U.S. Patent No. 7,258,559 (June 15, 2005).

Glenn Michael Richards
Curriculum vitae
Page 3

RESEARCH EXPERIENCE (2005) – Continued

Theses Supervised (Major Advisor)
- 18. Harold J. Niemeyer. Discriminative stimulus properties of hallucinogens and related designer drugs, Ph.D. in Pharmaceutical Sciences awarded May 2005.

PUBLICATIONS (2005)

Articles in Peer-reviewed Journals
- 274. Richards GM, Long RA, Johnson TE, Bunker PY. 2-Substituted tryptamines: Agents with selectivity for 5-HT6 receptors. *J. Med. Chem.* 48:1042-1049, 2005.
- 273. Young SC, Richards GM, Fong AN, Khun PK, Davis HW, Bond CK, Gerber HD. (+) Amphetamine stimulus generalization to an herbal ephedrine product. *Pharmacol. Biochem. Behav.* 70: 445-448, 2005.
- 272. Martin WR, Constantine DV, Jacobs IL, Sessler JL. Richards GM. A highly conserved aspartic acid (Asp-155) anchors the terminal amine moiety of tryptamines and is involved in membrane targeting of the 5-HT serotonin receptor. *J. Pharmacol. Exp. Ther.* 298: 884-889, 2005.
- 271. Heltzer NT, Richards GM, Ringley OC, Krueger TT. Central nicotinic receptor ligands and pharmacophores. *Pharm. Acta Helv.* 84:66-79, 2005.
- 270. Richards GM, Johnson TE, Jacobs IL. Binding of β-carbolines and related agents at serotonin (5-HT$_2$ and 5-HT$_{3C}$), dopamine and benzodiazepine receptors. *Psychopharmacology*. 155:305-316 (2005).
- 269. Sliaken VA, Washington PK, Richards GM, Darson KM. 1-[4-(2-Phenylalkyl)phenyl]-2-aminopropanes as 5-HT$_{3C}$ partial agonists. *J. Med. Chem.* 70: 786-794, 2005.
- 268. Wong XJ, Bond MI, Malhumariart RB, Richards GM. Binding of spiperone analogs at 5-HT$_{2A}$ serotonin receptors. *Eur. J. Pharmacol.* 389: 34-41, 2005.
- 267. Johnson TE, Fong AN, Richards GM, Gerber SN. Serotonin receptor binding or indolealkylamines: A preliminary structure-affinity investigation. *Med. Chem. Res.* 15: 128-134, 2005.

Invited Book Chapters
- 43. Richards GM. Neurobiology of hallucinogens, in *Handbook of Substance Abuse: Neurobehavioral Pharmacology*. Basel: Springer Verlag, 2005.

INVITED PRESENTATIONS (2005)

- 89. Serotonin receptor subtypes, 25th Annual International Symposium on Substance Abuse, Tokyo, Japan, May 2005.
- 88. Serotonin receptors and drugs affecting neurotransmission, University of Zurich, Zurich, Switzerland, March 2005.

Actual CV size is 8.5 x 11

Glenn Michael Richards
Curriculum vitae
Page 4

TEACHING EXPERIENCE (2005)

- MEDC-526, Research Techniques in Medicinal Chemistry, lecturer, Spring 2005.
- MEDC-603, Medicinal Chemistry II, course coordinator, Spring 2005.
- MEDC-604, Medicinal Chemistry III, lecturer, Fall 2005.

SERVICE ACTIVITIES (2005)

National
- Member, National Advisory Council on Drug Abuse, Department of Health and Human Services, National Institutes of Health, National Institute on Drug Abuse
- Chair-elect, Medicinal and Natural Products Chemistry Section, American Association of Pharmaceutical Scientists
- Member, Awards Committee, American Association of Pharmaceutical Scientists

State
- Member, Georgia Council on Substance Abuse

University
- Member, Executive Budget Committee
- Vice-Chair, Health Sciences Research Space Advisory Committee
- Member, Search Committee for Chair of the Department of Chemistry

College
- Member, Strategic Planning Committee
- Member, Space Planning Committee
- Member, Academic Performance Committee
- Member, Scholarship and Awards Committee

PROFESSIONAL MEMBERSHIPS (2005)

- American Association of Colleges of Pharmacy
- American Pharmacists Association
- American Association of Pharmaceutical Scientists
- American Chemical Society
- American Association for the Advancement of Science
- Rho Chi Honor Society
- Phi Kappa Phi Honor Society

REFERENCES
Available upon request

Chapter 6

Developing a Portfolio

Artists and teachers have used portfolios for years to organize and document their professional growth. Pharmacy professionals can use these same techniques to highlight their progressive knowledge and skills. In fact, a portfolio gives a "show and tell" perspective of your experience and accomplishments. Just as you add information to your résumé and curriculum vitae, make a habit of adding to your portfolio samples of your work and examples of your achievements as you progress in your career. Items for inclusion might be details about your experiential training, project samples, summaries, credentials, and photos.

> A portfolio gives a "show and tell" perspective of your experience and accomplishments.

Portfolio Design

How you design your portfolio will depend on the intended audience. Always include examples of your work that highlight the knowledge and skills relevant to the position you seek. Also, include an outline or index of the information in your portfolio. This will convey a neat, concise, and professional image.

Keep in mind that it's a portfolio, not a scrapbook, so avoid making it "cute" and stick to businesslike graphics, headers, colors, and text fonts. This is not the place for hot pink paper or photos mounted on doilies. Office supply stores sell binders and zippered portfolio cases in which you can insert transparent, three-hole-punched sheet protectors to display your materials.

Because of the large amount of information contained in a typical portfolio, you may want to consider having an electronic version available on CD-ROM or through the Internet. This way you can easily mail a CD-ROM or supply the link to your Web-based portfolio when prospective employers express an interest in seeing it.

Representative Components of a Portfolio

Personal Information

Begin your portfolio with your résumé or curriculum vitae. Consider including a personal statement that reflects your goals and objectives. If desired, this statement can summarize your commitment to a professional practice philosophy, teaching philosophy, or research and scholarship philosophy.

To enhance the personal nature of your portfolio, you may want to include a photograph and provide a list of your mentors and how they have assisted in your professional development. Including a list of your personal interests reflects your ability to balance work and leisure time.

Education

You may find it helpful include a separate section in your portfolio for your education. List the universities and colleges that you attended along with the degree or degrees you earned. If you completed a graduate degree, describe your graduate thesis and provide a brief biographical sketch of your major professor. You can also include transcripts from your college work as well as a photograph of your diploma.

Experiential Learning

All pharmacists acquire experiential learning as part of fulfilling their degree requirements. This can range from internships to post graduate training experiences. Depending on your stage of professional development, you may want to amplify the most current training areas.

For example, a pharmacy student could list internships and advanced practice experience (i.e., clerkships) along with the name of the practice site, preceptor, description of duties and responsibilities, and preceptor evaluations.

EDUCATIONAL OUTCOMES A PORTFOLIO CAN HIGHLIGHT

1. **Pharmaceutical Care.** Provide pharmaceutical care in cooperation with patients, prescribers, and other members of an interprofessional health care team based on sound therapeutic principles and evidence-based data, taking into account relevant legal, ethical, social, economic, and professional issues, emerging technologies, and evolving biomedical, sociobehavioral, and clinical sciences that may impact therapeutic outcomes.

   a. Provide patient-centered care.

      - Design, implement, monitor, evaluate, and adjust patient-specific and evidence-based pharmaceutical care plans.
      - Communicate and collaborate with prescribers, patients, caregivers, and other health care providers to engender a team approach to patient care.
      - Retrieve, analyze, and interpret the professional, lay, and scientific literature to provide drug information to patients, their families, and other health care providers.
      - Carry out duties in accordance with legal, ethical, social, economic, and professional guidelines.
      - Maintain professional competence by identifying and analyzing emerging issues, products, and services that may impact patient-specific therapeutic outcomes.

   b. Provide population-based care.

      - Develop and implement population-specific, evidence-based disease management programs and protocols based on analysis of epidemiologic and pharmacoeconomic data, medication use criteria, medication use review, and risk reduction strategies.
      - Communicate and collaborate with prescribers, population members, care givers, and other health care providers to engender a team approach to patient care.
      - Retrieve, analyze, and interpret the professional, lay, and scientific literature to provide drug information to other health care providers and the public.
      - Carry out duties in accordance with legal, ethical, social, economic, and professional guidelines.
      - Maintain professional competence by identifying and analyzing emerging issues, products, and services that may impact population-based, therapeutic outcomes.

2. **Systems Management.** Manage and use resources of the health care system in cooperation with patients, prescribers, other health care providers, and administrative and supportive personnel to promote health; provide, assess, and coordinate safe, accurate, and time-sensitive medication distribution; and improve therapeutic outcomes of medication use.

   a. Manage human, physical, medical, informational, and technological resources.

      - Apply relevant legal, ethical, social, economic, and professional principles/issues to ensure efficient, cost-effective use of human, physical, medical, informational, and technological resources in the provision of patient care.
      - Communicate and collaborate with patients, prescribers, other health care providers, and administrative and supportive personnel to engender a team approach to ensure efficient, cost-effective use of human, physical, medical, informational, and technological resources in the provision of patient care.
      - Carry out duties in accordance with legal, ethical, social, economic, and professional guidelines.
      - Maintain professional competence by identifying and analyzing emerging issues, products, and services that may impact management of human, physical, medical, informational, and technological resources in the provision of patient care.

   b. Manage medication use systems.

      - Apply patient- and population-specific data, quality assurance strategies, and research processes to ensure that medication use systems minimize drug misadventuring and optimize patient outcomes.
      - Apply patient- and population-specific data, quality assurance strategies, and research processes to develop drug use and health policy, and to design pharmacy benefits.
      - Communicate and collaborate with prescribers, patients, caregivers, other health care providers, and administrative and supportive personnel to identify and resolve medication use problems.

EDUCATIONAL OUTCOMES A PORTFOLIO CAN HIGHLIGHT *continued*

- Carry out duties in accordance with legal, ethical, social, economic, and professional guidelines.
- Maintain professional competence by identifying and analyzing emerging issues, products, and services that may impact medication use systems so as to develop health policy and design pharmacy benefits.

3. **Public Health.** Promote health improvement, wellness, and disease prevention in cooperation with patients, communities, at-risk populations, and other members of an interprofessional team of health care providers.

   a. Ensure the availability of effective, quality health and disease prevention services.
      - Apply population-specific data, quality assurance strategies, and research processes to develop, identify, and resolve public health problems.
      - Communicate and collaborate with prescribers, policy makers, members of the community, other health care providers, and administrative and supportive personnel to identify and resolve public health problems.
      - Carry out duties in accordance with legal, ethical, social, economic, and professional guidelines.
      - Identify and analyze emerging issues, products, and services that may affect the efficacy or quality of disease prevention services so as to amend existing or develop additional services.

   b. Develop public health policy.
      - Apply population-specific data, quality assurance strategies, and research processes to develop public health policy.
      - Communicate and collaborate with prescribers, policy makers, members of the community, and other health care providers and administrative and supportive personnel to develop public policy.
      - Carry out duties in accordance with legal, ethical, social, economic, and professional guidelines.
      - Identify and analyze emerging issues, products, and services that may affect public health policy so as to amend existing or develop additional policies.

Source: Adapted from the American Association of Colleges of Pharmacy's Center for the Advancement of Pharmaceutical Education. Educational Outcomes, 2004.

Use discretion in including evaluations, however, since you want to provide a favorable impression of your performance.

A pharmacy resident may choose to describe residency rotations and to eliminate extensive information about advanced practice experiences gained as a pharmacy student. After practicing for several years, you can simply list these experiences in your curriculum vitae.

Recognition

Describing any kind of recognition you have received adds value to your portfolio. If you have received an award, for example, provide the title and a few words indicating its purpose, such as "for community service". You can enhance this listing by including a photograph of you receiving the recognition, a news clip, or a visual image of the actual award.

Licensure/Certification

Pharmacy technicians, students, and practicing pharmacists all must have specific certifications or licenses for employment in a pharmacy. In this section of the portfolio, you can describe such certifications and even include a photograph of the documents. Or, you can include a letter from an accrediting agency documenting your completion of a specific course or examination.

Professional Development

Position Summaries

Highlight your professional development by including information about positions you have held. Provide summary statements about specific positions or include copies of the position description. Additionally, consider adding a summary of your performance evaluations or a copy of these documents.

Service, Teaching, and Research

The service, teaching, and research triad can serve as a template for organizing your activities related to professional development. Focus areas can range from patient care to professional leadership.

If you are involved in teaching, include relevant samples. A preceptor can describe his or her advanced practice experience and provide copies of student evaluations. For faculty members, this section can include course syllabi, peer reviewer comments about teaching, lecture outlines, videotaped presentations, and samples of student assignments.

Research or scholarly activities will vary with your background. For some people, such as faculty members, this section may include information about grants, publications, and invited presentations. For others, the section might include an article prepared for a newsletter or the outline of a technician training program prepared for a community college course.

National Pharmacy Standards

Still another approach involves organizing your professional development section around specific standards published by national pharmacy organizations. For example, a pharmacy resident can match his or her knowledge and skills against published standards for the specific type of residency program, then indicate how he or she met each competency. Likewise, a pharmacy student can correlate knowledge and skills with the educational outcomes developed by either the American Association of Colleges of Pharmacy's Center for the Advancement of Pharmaceutical Education or the professional competencies and outcome expectations required by the Accreditation Council for Pharmacy Education. The box on pages 78-79 outlines some of these outcomes.

Memberships and Activities

The professional development area can also include a listing or description of your professional memberships, professional activities, areas of professional interests, consulting, and continuing education efforts.

Skills

Leadership

Most employers and program directors like to see evidence of leadership ability. You can demonstrate leadership potential by describing any elected or appointed positions you have held. Also, participation on a committee or team charged with completing a specific objective can show leadership abilities.

Communication

Effective communication skills are critical in every facet of the profession. Make sure you document evidence of your writing, speaking, and interpersonal communication successes. Include examples of oral presentations, written works, and situations where you've demonstrated strong interpersonal skills.

Information Technology

Technology continues to advance rapidly in the health care profession. To show potential employers you stay current with these changes, consider documenting your information technology skills. Describe your software proficiencies and explain how you apply technology in your teaching, research, and service activities.

Patient Care

Practicing pharmacists should consider highlighting their patient care skills. For example, document specific patient cases where your problem-solving skills and professional intervention resulted in a positive outcome. You can also compare your skills in disease state management with the competency statements of the National Institute for Standards in Pharmacist Credentialing (found at **www.nispcnet.org**).

Management

Documenting evidence of budgetary involvement and human resource experience can help show management experience, especially if you seek work in this setting.

References

Include a list of references in your portfolio. Rather than merely listing names and contact information, you may want to describe the significance of each reference you list. For example, explain your relationship with each person and the type of insight he or she can provide. Also, consider requesting general letters of reference from colleagues and mentors to include in your portfolio.

PORTFOLIO COMPONENTS

1. Personal Information
   - Name, designation, and title.
   - Contact information.
   - Mentors.
   - Résumé or curriculum vitae.
   - Personal Statement.
   - Photograph.
   - Personal interests.

2. Education
   - College or university attended.
   - Degree(s) awarded.
   - Major(s).
   - Graduate thesis and major professor.
   - Academic record or transcript(s).

3. Licensure/Certification
   - Pharmacy licensure information.
   - Specialty practice certification.
   - Certificates of completion.

4. Experiential Learning
   - Internship.
   - Advanced practice experiences.
   - Residency.
   - Fellowship.
   - Fulfillment of standards created by national organizations.

5. Recognition
   - Scholarships.
   - Academic honors.
   - Awards.
   - Certificates recognizing achievement.
   - Letters recognizing achievement.

6. Professional Development
   - Positions held and descriptions of duties.
   - Performance evaluations.
   - Service
     - Patient care.
     - Community.
     - School.
     - University.
     - Professional.
   - Teaching
     - Lecture titles.
     - Courses developed with syllabi.
     - Courses coordinated with syllabi.
     - Student evaluations.
     - Peer reviewer comments.
     - Sample of lecture outlines/slide presentations.
     - Videotape of lecture(s) or segment(s).
     - Self-evaluation and description of improvement.
     - Instructional strategies.
     - Samples of students' work (e.g., exams, papers, projects).
   - Research/Scholarship
     - Areas of interest/expertise.
     - Grants.
     - Contracts.
     - Projects.
   - Publications
     - Abstracts.
     - Articles.
   - Presentations
     - Letters of invitation.
     - Presentation evaluations.
     - Sample handouts, slides, videos.
     - Posters.
   - Professional memberships.
   - Professional activities.
   - Professional interests.
   - Consulting.
   - Continuing education.

7. Skills
   - Leadership
     - Elected positions.
     - Appointed positions.
     - Committee participation.
     - Agendas.
     - Documentation of outcomes.
     - Team involvement.
   - Communication
     - Oral presentations.
     - Written works.
     - Interpersonal skills.
   - Computer
     - Software proficiency.
     - Application of technology in teaching, research, and service.
   - Professional practice
     - Patient case discussions.
     - Evidence of problem solving.
   - Management
     - Budget preparation.
     - Human resource management.

8. References
   - List of references and the significance of their relationship.
   - Letters from colleagues.

Chapter 7

Presenting a Professional Image

Whenever you meet someone new, that person forms a first impression of you. Good or bad, these impressions last a long time.

As a pharmacy professional, you must remain aware of your professional image at all times. Your appearance, communications (written, verbal, and nonverbal), and manners represent major components of your professional image.

This chapter gives an overview of professionalism that you can use as a framework for guiding and enhancing your professional development. The chapter then covers two major obstacles to presenting a professional image during interviews and other encounters—nonverbal communication and dining etiquette—and includes tips for succeeding in these areas.

Professionalism

You demonstrate your professionalism each day by the way you look, think, and act. Throughout your career, your professional reputation will be one of your biggest assets, opening doors and providing opportunities in a way that nothing else can—not a perfect résumé, prestigious education, or impressive employment history.

Pharmacists' ethical traits—a key component of professionalism—are rated so highly in annual surveys that they serve as a model for all members of the health care community. In fact, although pharmacists always score at or near the top when Gallup surveys the public about how it perceives the ethics and honesty of key professions, pharmacists were rated more highly in the most recent poll (2004) than at any time in the past 20 years.[1]

Professionalism is an elusive concept. As Dana P. Hammer, director of the Pharmaceutical Care Learning Center at the University of Washington, noted in an article on professionalism published in 2000,[2] "You know it when you see it. You certainly know when you see its antithesis. And you know it when you are expecting to see it, but do not." Hammer points out that although professionalism is difficult to measure, "It can determine success in one's career, as well as elevate or erode one's occupation or profession."

Members of the pharmacy profession embody the concept of "professionalism" by sharing many common characteristics, according to a White Paper on pharmacy student professionalism published in 2000.[3] In addition to knowledge and skills, these traits include trustworthiness, accountability, ethically sound decision-making, and leadership. The sections below provide an overview of the professional traits expected of you as a pharmacist.

Knowledge and Skills

Pharmacy professionals display knowledge and competence in their unique areas of expertise. They follow professional norms and behaviors. They communicate effectively and use critical thinking to solve problems.

NONVERBAL CUES

- Make direct eye contact, especially at the time of an introduction.

- A sincere smile conveys confidence and a positive outlook. Remember that a negative facial expression can easily negate a positive message.

- Members of the profession usually shake hands upon meeting. Give a firm hand shake with two short shakes. Practice shaking hands with colleagues to perfect the skill.

PROFESSIONAL DRESS FOR WOMEN

- Professional dress for women usually begins with a comfortable skirted suit in a conservative color such as black, blue, brown, or beige accompanied by a tailored blouse in a contrasting solid color or muted print.

- A conservative pump with a short and closed heel and closed toe provides your best shoe choice, especially since many interview sessions involve tours or walking to meet with various interviewers.

- Keep accessories such as jewelry, scarves, and hosiery conservative.

- Minimize or eliminate atypical body adornments such as multiple earrings in one or both ears. Consider masking any tattoos, if possible.

- Seek professional advice for your hair style.

- Keep your makeup muted and avoid strong fragrances.

- Keep your nails clean and preferably short. Use only muted colored nail polish.

- Carry a small attaché or portfolio along with your purse, if necessary.

Commitment to Self-Improvement

Pharmacy professionals accept and respond to constructive feedback and seek opportunities for improvement. They recognize their limitations and seek assistance when necessary. They continually seek to improve their knowledge and skills throughout their lifetime.

Service Orientation/Altruism

Pharmacy professionals serve others. They provide service to their community and do not seek to profit unfairly from others. They put the needs of the patients they serve above their own.

Pride in the Profession

Pharmacy professionals demonstrate a strong work ethic and commitment to the profession. They are loyal, conscientious, and well prepared. They attempt to exceed expectations and strive for excellence.

Covenantal Relationship with Patients

Pharmacy professionals display compassion and empathy to patients and other caregivers. They respect a patient's privacy as well as their diversity of race, gender, religion, sexual orientation, age, disability, and socioeconomic status. They take time to explain information to patients and serve as advocates for those who cannot advocate for themselves.

Creativity and Innovation

Pharmacy professionals participate in activities which contribute to developing new knowledge and practice. They embrace change and apply creative and innovative approaches to challenges.

Accountability

Pharmacy professionals demonstrate initiative, reliability, and follow-through in fulfilling their commitments. They meet deadlines and complete their responsibilities in a timely manner. They accept responsibility for their errors and control their emotions appropriately, even under stressful conditions.

Ethically Sound Decision-Making

Pharmacy professionals display honesty and forthrightness when they interact with patients, peers, faculty, and other health professionals. They adhere to high ethical and moral standards. They cope with life's situations, despite a high degree of complexity and uncertainty.

Leadership

Pharmacy professionals contribute to the profession and actively participate in professional organizations. They take a proactive role in solving social issues. They help build and maintain a culture that promotes professionalism

Professional Presence

Members of the pharmacy profession have high professional expectations of their colleagues. As a result, you need to focus on your professional presence when seeking a pharmacy-related position. Professional presence has to do with hard-to-define social abilities, manners, and interpersonal skills. When someone has a professional demeanor, it inspires confidence in others and makes them feel good about the person's abilities. Bottom line—a good professional presence means creating a positive impression.

Begin by focusing on your nonverbal communication, including your eye contact, facial expressions, handshakes, and professional attire. Nonverbal communication is so powerful that even when you are saying one thing, people may interpret something else from your tone of voice or body language.

The first three boxes in this chapter contain important tips to remember about nonverbal communication. No matter how flamboyant or offbeat you like to be with your looks and behavior during "down time," the safest—and most professional—route is conservative.

Dining Etiquette

Most interview sessions involve one or more meals. As a result, you need to understand and follow established rules of dining etiquette. It may seem trivial, but proper etiquette for eating plays a significant role in making a good impression. That said, if you're unsure exactly what to do at some part of the meal, try to relax. Do what strikes you as logical and gracious.

Unfortunately, many interviewers do not wait for the conclusion of a meal to begin questioning applicants. This means that you will do most of the talking while the interviewer or interviewers savor their meal. Answering their questions takes top priority, so don't worry about finishing your food.

Most of your conversation will relate to pharmacy during an interview session or other discussion, although you may venture into small talk as well. Do not lose sight of good manners, no matter how enthusiastic you feel as the conversation turns to the Red Sox, Toots and the Maytals, or Brad Pitt. Knowing and applying appropriate social behavior remains imperative for a successful interview.

The following guidelines should help you appear confident and comfortable at any meal function.

PROFESSIONAL DRESS FOR MEN

- Professional dress for men usually begins with a pure wool or wool blend suit. Common colors include dark gray or dark blue, with or without a subtle pinstripe pattern. Make sure your coat sleeves end at the middle of your wrist bone. You can have your pants finished with either a cuff or plain bottom.

- Wear a long-sleeved, lightly colored dress shirt with a darker tie.

- Common types of ties include solid color silk ties or those with repeating patterns of geometric prints or stripes. Make sure your tie complements your suit.

- Properly tie your tie using a four-in-hand, Windsor, or half-Windsor knot. Your tie should hang down to the center of your belt buckle. You do not need to use a tie clip or pin. Avoid clip-on ties, unless you have a physical disability that limits your manual dexterity.

- Your dark leather belt and oxford style shoes should match in color.

- Wear freshly polished shoes.

- The color of your socks should match your shoes or your pants. Choose a conservative color and pattern. When in doubt, choose a solid black sock.

- Minimize or eliminate atypical body adornments such as earrings in one or both ears. Consider masking any tattoos.

- Keep your hair style conservative and trim any facial hair.

- Carry a small attaché or portfolio, if necessary.

TABLE MANNERS

Using good table manners helps create a positive impression in an interview. The list below contains basic—but very important—table manners for you to follow.

- Don't chew food with your mouth open.

- Don't talk with your mouth full.

- Keep your elbows away from the table surface by eating with one hand and placing the other on your lap.

- Avoid seasoning your food before tasting it.

- Don't chew ice.

- Don't pour coffee or tea from your saucer into your cup.

- Chew and swallow your food before taking a drink of any liquid.

- Say "no, thank you" to the wait staff instead of turning your cup or wine glass over if you do not want coffee or wine.

- Always ask others to pass items to you rather than reaching across the table.

- Pass food and other items to the right.

- Pass the salt and pepper together.

- Pass the gravy or salad dressing vessel with the handle of the ladle facing the receiving individual.

- Ask for a replacement if you drop your flatware or napkin.

- Do not use a toothpick to clean your teeth.

Beginning the Meal

- Turn your cell phone off before arriving at the restaurant. Never answer your cell phone at the table.

- Leave your purse or attaché or other items under your chair.

- Place your napkin on your lap, either after your host does so or when handed to you by a server.

- Select a medium-priced entrée.

- When everyone at the table has been served, follow the lead of your host to begin eating.

During the Meal

- If you leave the table during the meal, put your napkin on the seat of your chair or to the left of your plate.

- Avoid sharing food, even if offered.

- Use discretion in drinking alcoholic beverages.

- Don't smoke at the table, even if you are in a smoking section of a restaurant.

- Avoid complaining about the food or service.

Special Protocol

The Place Setting

The place setting will vary with the formality of the meal. In general, a place setting consists of a plate in the center with forks, napkin, and bread and butter plate on the left. A knife, teaspoon, soup spoon, glasses for water and wine, and cup and saucer get positioned to the right. You may find a dessert fork and spoon at the top of the dinner plate. See Figure 7.1 for a view of the typical place setting.

It's amazing how many people are confused about what each plate and utensil is for. Typically you start with those on the outside, and work your way in. When in doubt about how to proceed, observe your host or take cues from others at the table.

Foods to Avoid

- Avoid making an issue about your special dietary needs (e.g., allergies, religious observances, vegetarian), since most restaurants have a variety of food choices.

- Consider saying "no, thank you" when offered soup, especially if you have a tendency to spill food.

- Avoid long pasta such as spaghetti or linguine.

Utensils

- Select your flatware from the outside in as the meal progresses.

- Use your fork and knife in the American style by holding the knife in your right hand and fork in your left hand with the fork tines piercing the food. After cutting a bite-size portion of food, lay your knife across the top edge of your plate with the sharp edge facing you. Change the fork to your right hand with the fork tines facing up. See Figure 7-2 on the next page for a visual example.

- Use your knife—not your fingers—to push food onto your fork.

- Using your knife, cut one bite-size portion of food at a time.

- Use your knife and salad fork to cut any large piece of salad just prior to eating.

- Never return a used piece of flatware to the table top.

Bread Plate

- Place a pat or two of butter on your bread plate and pass the butter to the person on your right before attempting to butter your bread.

- Remember that your bread plate stays on the left and liquids go on the right side of your plate. Servers remember this as solids on the left and liquids on the right.

- If the person to your left uses your bread plate by mistake, ask the server for another plate.

- Break a small portion of your bread prior to eating it and butter each portion beforehand rather than cutting or buttering all your bread at one time.

Soup

- When eating soup, push the spoon away from you rather than toward you before lifting the spoon to your mouth.

- Don't slurp when eating your soup or blow on hot soup.

Figure 7.1 Typical Place Setting

A. Dinner Plate
B. Soup Bowl
C. Bread Plate
D. Napkin
E. Salad Fork
F. Dinner Fork
G. Dinner Knife
H. Teaspoon
I. Soup Spoon
J. Butter Knife
K. Dessert Fork
L. Dessert Spoon
M. Water Glass
N. Wine Glass (Red)
O. Wine Glass (White)
P. Coffee/Tea Cup and Saucer

- Don't leave your spoon in a cup or bowl. Instead, place it on the side of the saucer or plate beneath the bowl.

Finishing the Meal

- You don't need to eat everything on your plate, especially if you are responding to multiple questions from interviewers.

- At the completion of your meal, consider your plate as the face of a clock. Leave the knife (blade facing inward) and fork (tines down) with the sharp ends of each pointing toward 10 and the flat ends pointing toward 4 (see Figure 7.3). This configuration lets the server know you're done.

- Do not move your plate when you finish and do not stack plates for the server.

- When you finish your meal, place your napkin on either side of your plate, although the right side is considered most acceptable. If a waiter has removed the plate, place your napkin in the center of the plate area. Don't place your napkin on your plate.

- Don't request a doggy bag for any unfinished food.

References

1. Carroll J. Honesty ratings of pharmacists, state officeholders reach new highs. The Gallup Organizaton. Available at: www.gallup.com/poll/content/login.aspx?ci=14290. Accessed July 18, 2005.

2. Hammer DP. Professional attitudes and behaviors: the "A's and B's" of professionalism. *Am J Pharm Educ*. 2000:64(4):455-64. Available at: http://www.ajpe.org/legacy/ajpe metaview.asp?ID=341. Accessed August 8, 2005.

3. Anon. White Paper on Pharmacy Student Professionalism. *J Am Pharm Assoc*. 2000;40:96-102.

Figure 7.2 Holding Fork American Style

Figure 7.3 Utensil Finished Position

Chapter 8

Introduction to Searching and Interviewing

The old saying, "You only get one chance to make a good first impression" conveys why it's critical to prepare for the interview process. Interviews give you the opportunity to communicate your knowledge, skills, abilities, and interests to potential employers, admissions personnel at educational institutions, and others in a position to make decisions that affect your future. With so much hanging on one interaction, you don't want to wing it.

Interviews also give you a chance to gather information about an employer or institution. Basically, they provide a way for both parties to determine the suitability of a match.

> Interviews allow job candidates and employers to assess the suitability of a match. You get the opportunity to highlight your knowledge, skills, abilities, and interests and to gather useful information about the employer or institution.

To make the most of your interview, you need to do your homework. First, ferret out the most worthwhile opportunities for you. Then ready yourself for interviews that cast your strengths in the best possible light and tell you what you need to know about the potential employer. Chapter 9 provides more extensive information on preparing for the interview.

Your Personal Marketing Materials

Before beginning your search, update all the documents you plan to use. Proofread all your documents—from your business card through your portfolio—to ensure current, consistent, and accurate information.

When seeking a position, you may need to use a combination of materials. The diagram below shows some of the tools you might use during your search and interview process.

Routinely, you will need a letter of introduction and a résumé or curriculum vitae. Also, you may want to prepare an elementary presentation portfolio consisting of your business card, career statement, and curriculum vitae. You can also create a cover letter that includes a link to your electronic portfolio.

The personal marketing documents you decide to use should depend on the situation. Too much information in an initial contact may overwhelm a potential employer. Instead, use an incremental approach. For example, you can use a cover letter and curriculum

Figure 8.1 Continuum of Personal Marketing Materials

Business Card → Résumé → Curriculum Vitae → Electronic Portfolio vitae for introductory purposes. At the time of an interview, you might provide an elementary presentation portfolio or a copy of your portfolio on a CD-ROM accompanied by your business card.

Requesting References

Selecting which references to use depends on the type of position you seek. Some employers or program directors will ask you to provide a set number of references, while others will indicate specific numbers and types of references. When providing references, keep the following points in mind:

- Give careful thought to the position description and attempt to match prospective references with the type of position.

- Contact your references ahead of time, or meet with them personally to explain the potential position and its importance to you.

- Provide each reference person with a copy of your résumé, curriculum vitae, or portfolio to ensure the accuracy of any details they might include in a reference letter. Also include a copy of the position description or other specifics about the potential position.

PREPARING A BUSINESS CARD

A business card is a convenient and inexpensive marketing tool. When you meet decision makers at networking events, educational sessions, and conferences, presenting them with your business card in a courteous, professional way may help to fix your name in their mind.

Your card should be clean and professional. The standard dimensions of 2 x 3.5 inches require that you be selective in your wording and design so the card is not overcrowded. The usual type size varies from 8 point to 11 point; the key is to make sure it is readable. If you work for a corporation or organization, it may specify the images and color that must be used. Otherwise, keep the card simple by using black ink on 100 pound professional white, off-white, or cream card stock. A horizontal format is most common for health professionals, as shown on the samples to the right.

Common information for your business card includes:

- Name
- Title
- Organization street address
- Alternate or home mailing address
- City and state abbreviation
- Zip + four mailing code
- Telephone number
- Alternate or mobile telephone number
- Fax number
- E-mail address

You can store the same information in your personal digital assistant (PDA) to create an electronic business card. This allows you to quickly beam your contact information to another person who has a similar device equipped with an infrared port. Since some PDAs and handheld devices cannot communicate with other brands, you may choose to install software on your device to eliminate electronic transfer problems. Examples of this type of software can be found at www.conduits.com.

Jennifer H. Kneeley
Doctor of Pharmacy Candidate
Class of 2007
School of Pharmacy

Virginia Commonwealth University

MCV Campus
410 North 12th Street
P.O. Box 980581
Richmond, Virginia 23298-0581

331-459-6770
jhkneele@vcu.edu

Ted Barker, R.Ph.
572 North Dewey
North Platte, NE 69101

Phone: 308-564-7000
Fax: 308-564-7100
tbarker@source.net

- Some reference forms may give you the option to waive your right to future access to the recommendation letter. Waiving this right shows employers you have trust and confidence in the recommender.

- In some cases, potential employers will contact references directly. Make certain that you list the current contact information for your references, especially telephone numbers and e-mail addresses.

- At the completion of the process, send a thank you note to those preparing references and tell them of your search outcome.

Search Techniques

Networking

The network of contacts you have established throughout your life can provide invaluable help in your search process. Key contacts include friends and acquaintances you interact with in your daily activities as well as people you know through past or current employment. Other valuable sources are faculty and classmates from education or training you have received. People you meet through organizational activities, especially those connected to the profession, can also help.

In the pharmacy profession, personal networks typically bring much better results than traditional means in helping people find opportunities that fit well with their interests and strengths. For example, a mentor may know about a new position that has not yet been advertised. Or, a colleague may connect you with his or her network of associates in another geographic area.

Put the word out to your peers and mentors—people you trust and respect—that you are exploring a job change or seeking a specific kind of opportunity. Even if they have no suggestions at the moment, they can serve as sounding boards and keep their antennae up for useful possibilities.

Advertisements

To some extent, the approach you follow for finding potential jobs depends on the type of position you seek. One common strategy involves reviewing advertisements in newspapers, professional newsletters, and journals. Due to the time delay associated with print media, however, only routine staff positions get announced this way. Because newspaper readership soars on Sundays, it's the best day of the week to check the employment section for positions in the health professions. Some employers prefer to target newspapers with the greatest circulation within a state or region, so don't rely on your hometown paper alone.

Advertisements in newsletters and journals published by professional organizations generally have the greatest time delay. As a result, they are not the best way for employers to announce entry-level positions they need to fill quickly. Since newsletters and journals have an extensive and focused readership, they are useful for announcing nationwide searches for management and specialist positions and highlighting positions that have remained vacant for a long time.

Plenty of other sources exist for printed job announcements, including flyers and listings at pharmacy schools. Schools and colleges often help employers announce positions to students and alumni. Usually, the dean's office or alumni staff can provide this information to students.

Placement Services

Many state and national pharmacy organizations offer placement services. These services vary from merely posting available positions for attendees to review (common at state meetings) to linking employers and applicants through a more structured process (more typically found at national meetings). Placement services at professional meetings routinely connect prospective graduate students, residents, and fellows with programs in their area of interest.

State and national organizations often maintain electronic databases of prospective employers and applicants, usually as a membership service or for an additional fee. Thanks to the Internet, this area has exploded, and many commercial placement services have sprung up as well. Most likely, pharmacy organizations' placement services can best meet your needs, since they have the clout and visibility to attract listings from top employers.

Career Day Events

Career day events are a popular way to recruit new graduates for employment or postgraduate training. Most schools and colleges hold such forums once a year. Similar to the placement services at state and national meetings, prospective employers visit the campus to interview graduating students for internships and employment. These visits provide a great opportunity for students seeking local and regional opportunities. Typically, you can sign up a few days in advance or that day for on-site interviews with representatives from various companies and organizations.

The Internet

The Internet offers an unsurpassed announcement method because of the immediacy of position listings, around-the-clock search availability, and convenience. Opportunities posted on the Internet commonly get announced through other communication channels, but the Internet gives you a quick, easy way to find a wealth of choices.

Some general sites promote health professional recruitment for many disciplines. Other sites tend to focus on specific employers or specific types of positions. Table 8.1 provides a sample listing of Internet sites.

Because the Internet constantly changes, some of these addresses may not stay valid. You can find other useful sites by keying the type of employment you desire into popular search engines, such as Google.

If a particular company or institution interests you, visit its Web site to obtain information about employment opportunities. Most Web pages have an easily identified icon indicating the link to position openings.

Professional Recruiters

Professional recruiters serve as intermediaries between employers and prospective employees. Most get paid by the employer after filling a specific position. Firms accepting contingency fees only receive payment when an individual gets hired.

Some recruiters arrange a direct fee-for-service agreement with the prospective employee. Most of the time you can probably find worthwhile opportunities without using a recruitment firm, but this route may make sense if you seek an upper-level management position or need to relocate to a geographic area where you don't have a professional network in place.

In general, a recruiter focuses on locating an applicant who meets the exact qualifications specified by an employer, rather than attempting to find the ideal position for you. Look for a reputable recruitment firm with a long-standing record. Before signing a contract, ask for references—a list of pharmacists you can contact who have used the service. You might also consider asking the firm to send you a copy of its code of ethics.

Table 8.1 Internet Sources for Position Listings

Organization	URL
America's Health Care Source	www.healthcaresource.com
America's Job Bank	www.ajb.dni.us
American College of Clinical Pharmacy	www.accp.com
American Pharmacists Association	www.aphanet.org
American Society of Health-System Pharmacists	www.ashp.org
Apogee Career Search	www.apogeemedicaljobs.com
Bio Online	www.bio.com
BioSource International	www.biosource.com
Career Builder	www.careerbuilder.com
Chase Group, Inc.	www.chasegroup.com
Chem Jobs	www.chemjobs.net
Clinical Research Job-Site	www.centerwatch.com
College Grad	www.collegegrad.com
Educational Directories Unlimited, Inc.	www.gradschools.com
Graduate Guide	www.graduateguide.com
Health Care Jobs Online	www.hcjobsonline.com
Health Care Job Store, Inc.	www.pharmacistjobs.com
Healthnet Professionals Network, Inc.	www.healthnetpro.com
Hire Health	www.hirehealth.com
Hire Med	www.hiremed.com
International Pharmajobs	www.pharmajobs.com
Job Engine	www.jobengine.com
Job Bank USA	jobbankusa.com
Job Hunt	www.job-hunt.org
Jobvertise	www.jobvertise.com

continued on page 93

Interview Basics

Doing Your Research

Before going on an interview, you need to learn as much as you can about the company or institution. Manuals on interviewing always tell you to evaluate your strengths and weaknesses beforehand so that you can effectively promote your assets. Likewise, you should review the strengths and weaknesses of the potential employers you have identified in your search process. Gather annual reports, company brochures, newspaper and magazine articles, information from the company Web sites, and material posted on other Web sites.

The reference librarian at your local or college library can help tremendously as you look for information on prospective companies. Read the material carefully. Note the facts presented, the questions raised, the positive aspects revealed, and the concerns planted in your mind. With this information in hand, you can prepare targeted questions for your interview.

Invitations to Interview

Employers do not usually invite you for an interview until you have provided sufficient background information, such as a fully completed application form and résumé or curriculum vitae. In large corporations, your information may get scanned electronically for keywords and screened by several people. In small companies, maybe only one or two people will sort through it.

Depending on the organization's size and recruitment strategy, a limited number of applicants will get invited for an interview. Most organizations handle invitations by telephone so that they can arrange a mutually convenient appointment. Organizations

Table 8.1, *continued* **Internet Sources for Position Listings**

Organization	URL
Management Recruiters of Portland, Oregon	www.mrportland.com
MedBulletin	medbulletin.com
MedHunters	medhunters.com
Medical Staffing Network	www.msnpharmacy.com
Med Options USA	www.medoptions.com
Medical Jobs Online	medicaljobsonline.com
MegaJobs Network Medical Jobs Finder	pharmacistjobsite.com
Monster	www.medsearch.com
National Association of Chain Drug Stores	www.nacds.org
NationJob Network	www.nationjob.com
Pharmaceutical Careers	www.pharmaceuticalcareers.com
Pharmacist Jobs	pharmacistjobs.com
Pharmacy Technician Certification Board	www.ptcb.org
PharmacyWeek	pharmacyweek.com
PharmWeb	www.pharmweb.net
RPh on the Go	rphonthego.com
RPh Professional Search	www.rphprosearch.com
Rx Career Center	rxcareercenter.com
SHS, Inc.	www.shsinc.com
Thomson Peterson's	www.petersons.com
United States Air Force	www.airforce.com
United States Army	www.goarmy.com
United States Food & Drug Administration	www.fda.gov
United States Navy	www.navy.com
United States Pharmacopeia	www.usp.org
United States Public Health Service	www.usphs.gov
University of Oklahoma College of Pharmacy	pharmacy.ouhsc.edu/index.asp

FINDING RESIDENCIES AND FELLOWSHIPS

For information about available positions for graduate students, residents, or fellows, you usually need to go directly to the sponsoring institution. Most maintain a Web site to describe their program offerings and admission requirements.

If you need help identifying programs, you can obtain a list of offerings from professional organizations such as:

Academy of Managed Care Pharmacy
100 North Pitt St., Suite 400
Alexandria, VA 22314
www.amcp.org
(800) 827-2627
(703) 683-8416

American Association of Colleges of Pharmacy
1426 Prince St.
Alexandria, VA 22314
www.aacp.org
(703) 739-2330

American Association of Pharmaceutical Scientists
2107 Wilson Blvd
Suite 700
Arlington, VA 22201
www.aaps.org
(703) 243-2800

American College of Clinical Pharmacy
3101 Broadway, Suite 380
Kansas City, MO 64111
www.accp.com
(816) 531-2177

American Pharmacists Association
2215 Constitution Ave., NW
Washington, DC
20037-2985
www.aphanet.org
(202) 628-4410

American Society of Consultant Pharmacists
1321 Duke St.
Alexandria, VA 22314
www.ascp.com
(800) 355-2727
(703) 739-1300

American Society of Health-System Pharmacists
7272 Wisconsin Ave.
Bethesda, MD 20814
www.ashp.org
(301) 657-3000

National Association of Chain Drug Stores
413 North Lee St.
P.O. Box 1417-D49
Alexandria, VA 22313-1480
www.nacds.org
(703) 549-3001

National Community Pharmacists Association
100 Daingerfield Rd.
Alexandria, VA 22314
www.ncpanet.org
(703) 683-8200

The National Pharmaceutical Association
107 Kilmayne Dr., Suite C
Cary, NC 27511
www.npha.net
(800) 944-6742

usually make these calls during working hours, so remember to provide a telephone number where prospective employers can reach you during the day. If you can only receive calls at home, make sure you have an answering machine or voice mail.

Screening Interviews

Potential employers commonly conduct initial screening interviews to identify the most promising candidates. In some organizations, staff from the human resources department handle these rather than pharmacy personnel. The screening interview usually lasts no longer than 30 minutes. The interviewer focuses on specific criteria to determine whether your knowledge and skills meet the position's requirements. He or she will also convey background information about the organization and position.

To gain a second interview, you need to project a positive image and present qualifications that fit well with the available position.

Quite often, screening interviews get conducted by telephone. Although impersonal, this approach offers an efficient and cost-effective solution, especially when long distances exist between you and the interviewer.

Sometimes screening interviews get videotaped. You might meet with a designated third party who will ask you a list of prepared questions and send the completed videotape to the interviewer.

Potential employers may also ask you to go to a convenient site with teleconferencing equipment, such as a local college or a business hotel, where they can interview you over a video monitor.

A much rarer approach—but likely to increase as the technology becomes more available—involves an electronic interactive interview. Using camcorder technology between your computer and the interviewer's, you can communicate and answer questions over the Internet.

Six Major Interview Formats

An interview can take many different formats. By preparing yourself for these different possibilities, you will gain a much stronger edge in the interview process.

1. **Behavioral Interview**. This type of interview looks at your past performance as a predictor of future success. Interviewers will ask open-ended questions to identify your problem-solving skills, accomplishments, and areas for improvement. They will also seek specifics about past events and your role in the events. This method of interviewing attempts to get responses to actual, not hypothetical situations.

   Ideally, you should respond to a situation-based question using a story about your actual experience. Expect a series of follow-up questions (e.g., What did you do next? How did you feel? What was your role? What were you thinking? What was the result?). In this type of interview, you must demonstrate actual results from your acquired experiences.

2. **Stress Interview**. In this approach, the interviewer typically uses intimidating verbal and nonverbal communications such as long periods of silence, avoiding eye contact, and challenging your comments in an aggressive or unfriendly way. The interviewer may even misinterpret your response to evoke a counter response. This kind of interview highlights when and how you assert yourself. Although not a common style of interviewing, you can succeed with this type of approach if you do not take the behavior of the interviewer personally.

3. **Group Interview**. Some organizations include several interviewers in a room with a single candidate—or several candidates together. Although applicants tend to find group interviews stressful, they can help employers determine how you interact outside of one-on-one situations.

In one type of group interview, interviewers will represent different personality characteristics, such as friendly, arrogant, and assertive. They then evaluate you on how well you handle the various styles while responding to specific questions. Another approach uses the peers you would work closely with—if hired—as the interviewers.

4. **Directive Interview**. This type of interview requires the interviewer to ask each candidate the same series of predetermined questions. The questions usually align with the specific tasks and duties of the position description. Although a rigid process, this type of interview gives you an opportunity to provide additional information when responding to each specific question.

5. **Case Study**. Yet another tack involves gathering several applicants in a room and having them complete a task or evaluate a case study. For example, the interviewer might ask you to design a therapeutic regimen for a patient with several chronic diseases or determine the best means of reducing prescription waiting time at a hypothetical pharmacy. As the group reviews the case study, conflicting views emerge and the interviewer assesses the applicants' styles in terms of problem-solving, decision-making, creativity, and the ability to work effectively on a team.

6. **Luncheon or Dinner Interview**. This type of interview assesses your performance in a social situation and gives interviewers the opportunity to continue with their evaluation of you as a prospect. Since this type of interview is often very intimidating, Chapter 7 includes tips for making the situation successful. Remember that some employers may use other social venues such as meetings or receptions to assess your social behavior.

THE THANK YOU NOTE

Always follow up your interview with a thank you note for both screening and selection interviews. In the case of a group interview, send a thank you note to everyone you met with, or at least to the primary interviewers.

Interviewers appreciate notes, which not only demonstrate good manners but also help remind interviewers who you are and what you offer. Sometimes a thank you note provides the extra something that makes you stand out from the crowd. For a personalized touch, write your note by hand using your best penmanship. Although popular, electronic messages are not the ideal way to send a personal thank you note.

An effective thank you note should:

- Remind the interviewer of the position you desire.

- Stress your interest in the position and the company.

- Emphasize one or two of your strongest skills, tailored to the interviewer's concerns.

- Include your contact information and the best times to reach you.

- Close with a suggestion for further action, such as a second meeting.

- Be brief—roughly a dozen sentences.

- Be free of spelling errors, typos, and other gaffes.

Don't let the note backfire on you by begging for the position or coming across as if you think you already have the job.

Selection Interviews

The second interview, often considered a selection interview, usually gets conducted by personnel with the authority to extend an offer if they decide you best fit the position. The interview may be one-on-one, a group meeting, or a combination of both. Some last a few hours; others take an entire day. During the session, interviewers will seek more information about your knowledge, skills, and professional experience. The interviewer may rely on specific questions pertaining to the position, or the interview may take the form of a casual conversation. The latter style encourages open communication and allows you to steer the discussion toward your strengths.

The box on page 95 details specific formats that interviewers may use to assess your qualifications and personal style.

Following the Interview

After the interview, prepare a personal summary of new information you learned during the session. In your notes, include perceptions of people you met, details about the environment, and facts about the position. Although you may think you'll clearly remember everything you saw and heard, memories fade. After several interviews, details from one site can get confused with those from another. Also, make sure you record the names of your interviewers, especially if they did not provide an itinerary.

Write a thank you note as soon as possible after the interview, preferably the same day. Address it to the primary interviewer, and include the names of any people you found especially helpful during the interview session. Keep the note positive and highlight your continuing interest in the position.

Chapter 9

The Interview:
Before, During, and After

Preparing for the Interview

Do Your Homework

Learning as much as you can about an organization before an interview will help you make the most of your time during the session. You will come across as thorough, professional, and highly interested in the position. Advance preparation also enables you to ask better questions, so you're more likely to get the information you need to evaluate the position.

To obtain background information, you can request it directly from the company during your preliminary discussions. The World Wide Web provides another excellent source. Use any common search engine to locate the company's Web address. Once you've found the Web site, look for the following information about the company:

- Location.
- Type of facilities.
- Organizational structure.
- Reputation.
- Personnel demographics.
- Scope of products or services provided.
- Strategic plan.
- Financial position.

You can find financial information in annual reports, public records, and on the Internet. In the case of for-profit corporations, stock brokerage firms can provide financial history information. Financial news periodicals and investment directories available online have excellent information and also provide links to other helpful sites.

Look for evidence of the company's financial viability. Important things to know include whether the company plans to expand, has soaring or plummeting stock value, or another company seeks to acquire it.

You can also search other sites and online publications for information about the company. For example, a magazine profile or newspaper articles can provide insights into a company's strengths, philosophy, future directions, and so on. Electronic resources such as Lexis-Nexis—which may be accessible through your local library or university—can retrieve recent articles that give you a sense of the company's focus and direction.

If you know any current or past employees of the companies you're interested in, they can provide an additional source of information. Ask them about the work atmosphere and look for insights into the organization's strengths and weaknesses. Remember, however, that their perspectives are subjective and limited to their own experiences. Round out your research with input from other sources so you're not relying strictly on one person's opinion.

Fill Out Application Forms

Before extending an interview invitation, many organizations require that you complete an application form. Remember these important points.

Provide Details

Follow instructions carefully and pay attention to detail as you fill out the form. Although your curriculum vitae should have most of the general information requested, resist the temptation of completing blanks by stating "see attached curriculum vitae." The application needs to stand on its own in case it becomes separated from the curriculum vitae. For example, some offices file applications in one place and CVs and background materials in another. Some scan applications and store the information electronically.

Filling out the application completely also conveys a message that you work thoroughly and conscientiously—and that you care enough about the position to do things correctly.

E-MAIL ETIQUETTE

Electronic messages have become an increasingly important part of interviewing communications. As a result, you must make sure your e-mail messages portray a professional image at all times. When drafting e-mail messages, remember these tips.

Do...

- Try to return e-mail messages in the same time period that you would for a telephone message.

- Use the same proper grammar, spelling, paragraph structure, and punctuation that you would for other written communications.

- Choose a subject line that accurately reflects your reason for communicating. Make it descriptive, such as "confirming our meeting tomorrow" instead of a label, such as "meeting."

- Set the text wrap feature (via the preferences option on your e-mail tool bar) at approximately 75 characters.

- Save your message in draft form and put it aside to review again before you send it. People tend to dash off e-mails quickly, which invites errors, so take the time to proofread carefully. If you receive a message that evokes an emotional response, such as anger or frustration, do not respond immediately.

- Remember that e-mail messages are public and long-lasting documents. Write as if the whole world will read your message.

- Try to keep your message brief (e.g., less than a page in length). Use concise wording and stay on topic.

- Keep the tone of your message friendly and professional.

- If you attach documents to supplement your message, tell the reader what you have attached. Understand that some people may not open attachments because of fear of viruses.

- Prepare a proper signature with your complete contact information.

Continued on page 99

List Employment History

Applications will ask for the beginning and ending dates of past employment. For each past position, list your employment dates and provide a brief statement explaining your reason for leaving. Try to cast your comments in a positive light, such as "to gain additional practice experience" or "to return to college on a full-time basis." Avoid negative statements.

Give Salary History

Some applications will request your salary or wage history. Make sure you have starting and ending figures for each position. Some employers may request this information on a per-hour basis, while others may request the same information as an annual amount.

Occasionally, an application form may request your salary or wage expectation. If this happens, ask colleagues about the organization's salary or wage structure. You can also get general information about salaries and wages by reviewing published advertisements that include salary ranges, talking with professional recruiters, and reviewing Internet sites. Some sites list specific salary and wage information (e.g., www.bls.gov, www.pharmacyweek.org, and www.wageweb.com). Others enable you to determine appropriate salaries according to the cost of living in selected geographic areas (e.g., www.homefair.com). To avoid listing a specific amount on the application, you can simply use the word "negotiable."

Remember, Neatness and Spelling Count

Keep your application neat and avoid typographical or spelling errors. If you need more space, append a sheet and carefully cross-reference your responses. Print your responses by hand or—for the best results—type them. Or, ask for a form that you can download from the Internet and complete on your computer. Then you can either print it out and return a paper copy or send it back electronically. You can also scan the paper application and complete it on your computer.

Complete all sections of the application. Use the words "none" or "not applicable" for sections that do not apply to you. For concerns about how requested information will get used, such as date of birth, marital status, dependents, disabilities, arrests, and convictions, talk with a representative of the nearest Equal Employment Opportunity Commission field office. Call 1-800-669-4000 for the number of a specific field office, or check the Web site at www.eeoc.gov.

As a final step, review the application for completeness and accuracy. Sign and date it and make a copy for your files. Unless you complete the application onsite, attach a cover letter before you turn it in.

Getting Ready

Practice, Practice, Practice

The interview gives you an opportunity to truly sell yourself. Review your résumé or curriculum vitae and practice responses to questions regarding your education, professional experience, and accomplishments. Chapter 10, entitled Interview Questions, provides more detail on questions interviewers frequently ask. Make sure your comments do not sound too "rehearsed." Also, think about tactful responses to inappropriate questions that inexperienced interviewers may ask you.

Conduct Mock Interviews

You may want to ask a colleague or mentor to conduct a mock interview to help you gain experience. Constructive feedback on your responses and delivery style can help you work out the kinks in advance.

Develop Question Lists

Most interviewers give you the opportunity to ask questions, so prepare a list of items you'd like to learn more about. Keep your questions geared toward helping you understand your scope of duties and how you would fit into the organization. Interviewers may become turned off by questions that seem irrelevant.

Remember Your Manners

It's a good idea to review books or articles on business etiquette and—if the interview involves lunch or dinner—table manners. You don't want to ruin a good impression by making a faux pas. Interviewers will look at both how you answer questions and how you conduct yourself overall.

Prepare for Presentations

Some interview sessions may call for a formal presentation. Faculty candidates, for example, may be asked to deliver a seminar. Make contact with the employer to determine the audience and get a general idea of their expectations. To ensure success in a formal presentation, make sure you prepare adequately and rehearse in advance.

Dress for Success

Appearance and grooming remain important elements of a successful interview. Project a professional image by wearing a dark-colored, conservative suit. Usually, dark blue, black, and gray are good color choices. Men should wear freshly shined dress shoes, while women should wear low-heeled pumps. Wear your hair in a neat and professional style. Avoid perfume, cologne, or aftershave.

E-MAIL ETIQUETTE

continued

Don't...

- Use emoticons (e.g., smiley faces) in professional communications.

- Use your personal e-mail address if the address doesn't sound professional (e.g., cutiepie@ centralcom.net).

- Attach extensive documents unless you can convert them to PDF files.

- React immediately to flaming (unprofessional, emotional, or rude) messages.

- Send personal information such as your social security number.

- Complete the "To" portion of the e-mail address until you have finalized your message, thus averting an unintentional "send."

- Mark every message as priority or urgent.

- Send repeat messages when you don't receive an immediate response to your initial message.

The Interview

Bring Applicable Documents

Bring along a slim briefcase, pad holder, or portfolio containing a copy of your résumé or CV, one or more lists of your references, and questions you can review when you are not actively interviewing.

Arrive on Time

Interviewers like punctuality. Arrive 10 to 15 minutes before your scheduled appointment, allowing you time to relax and collect your thoughts.

Use Nonverbal Communication Cues

From the outset, use appropriate nonverbal communication skills. Make eye contact, smile, and give the interviewer a firm handshake. Introduce yourself in a courteous manner. Avoid addressing your interviewers by first name unless they request otherwise. Do not sit down until the interviewer begins to sit or offers you a seat.

Maintain an enthusiastic and confident attitude at all times. Be alert and attentive—especially after lunch and during the late afternoon segment of a day-long interview, when energy tends to wane.

Remember Mealtime Etiquette

If your interview session includes a meal, pay particular attention to your dining etiquette. Choose your food carefully so that you can stay focused on your interviewer.

Avoid anything that has a tendency to splatter or might easily lodge in your teeth, including a messy pasta dish or a thick sandwich dripping with sauce.

Do not think of the meal as a gourmet experience—it's business. Chapter 7 has more tips—on dining etiquette.

Control Nervous Habits

Before your interview, ask friends or relatives if they've noticed that you have any nervous habits. Do you tend to chew on a fingernail? Lick your lips repeatedly? Twirl a lock of hair? Try to become conscious of anything you do that could be distracting or unprofessional, and avoid these behaviors during the interview. Also, avoid repeatedly injecting the word "like" or using slang expressions such as "awesome" or "yeah." Do not chew gum or smoke.

Use Effective Interpersonal Skills

Focus on using effective verbal and nonverbal interpersonal communication skills. Express yourself with clarity and precision. Use good listening skills, and remain tactful and respectful.

Interview Phases

Phase One: Establishing Rapport

A typical interview tends to take place in three phases. In the first phase, you and the interviewer establish rapport by discussing generic topics such as the weather or traffic conditions.

Phase Two: Asking Questions

The next phase involves the detailed part of the interview. It focuses on typical questions related to your qualifications and the position you seek. Listen carefully to the questions and do not hesitate to seek clarification. Answer questions honestly. Often, an interview session becomes a dialogue rather than the interviewer asking questions from a prepared list. A skilled interviewer will direct the discussion through focused questions, but will not dominate. Avoid rambling by keeping your comments to less than one minute per response. You can always take a moment to think about your answer to a specific question, and doing so avoids the appearance of giving a rehearsed response.

Watch for nonverbal cues from the interviewer, such as a raised eyebrow or a loud sigh. If you suspect that the interviewer isn't following you, ask, "Would you like me to clarify that?"

TIP: Give a firm handshake—not too tight or too limp. Pump the interviewer's hand twice and let go.

TOPICS TO AVOID DURING THE INTERVIEW

Failure to conform to certain interviewing norms will draw attention to your lack of savvy. Avoid these "red flags":

- Discussing salary and benefits early in the interview process.

- Consistently making references to the superiority of the institutions you're associated with.

- Speaking negatively about your current or past employers, faculty, or colleagues.

- Displaying a "know-it-all" attitude.

- Discussing religion, politics, or other highly controversial topics.

- Seeking special treatment because of your connections.

Phase Three: Summing it Up

In the final phase, the interviewer may recap key points and make statements such as "We've enjoyed having you here today" to signal that the interview is winding down. At this point, a good interviewer will ask if you have additional questions. This gives you the opportunity to seek more information and clarify any necessary points. You can also inquire about the timeline for completing the search process and when you may expect any follow-up.

If you are interested in the position, end the session by letting the interviewer know. Say that you enjoyed the meeting and look forward to the next step. As you take your leave, make eye contact, smile, and give the interviewer a firm handshake.

After the Interview

Assess the Experience

After completing the interview session, conduct a brief assessment. Record your personal observations about the environment, staff morale, advancement opportunities, and so on. Evaluate how well the position matches your expectations. How many of your essential attributes does the position provide? What points do you consider negotiable?

Also, conduct a self-assessment of your interviewing skills and identify areas for improvement. Do you feel happy with the way you answered specific questions? Did you get all the information you were looking for? Did you establish good rapport?

TIP: Don't tell interviewers what you can't do. Keep a positive attitude. Even if they ask you point blank, never say that you can't do something. Don't lie, of course. Simply elaborate on an experience that relates to the skill, or say that you're willing to learn.

Send a Thank You Note

Within two or three days, send a letter to your primary interview contact expressing thanks and noting your continued enthusiasm about the position. Consider letting other contacts in your network know about your interest in the position, especially if they have any close connections with the institution or organization.

Consider the Offer

After the interview process comes the nerve-wracking part of waiting for an acceptance or rejection. Employers often make rejections by mail and offers by phone. They will then follow up a verbal offer with a written letter that conveys important details.

Criteria to focus on as you consider various job offers include:

- How well your knowledge, skills, and abilities match your expectations for the position.

- The organization's size, management structure, reputation, opportunities for advancement, and work environment.

CELL PHONE ETIQUETTE

Many people forget to turn off their cell phones during an interview. And worse, when the phone rings, some people answer the call. Remember that interviewers will evaluate you during every stage of the interview process. Do not interrupt your interview to take calls from others. Play it safe by turning your cell phone off before you enter the office or building of the interview. Don't turn it on again until you're back on the street.

- Geographic location, including cost of living, housing availability, relocation expenses, and climate.

- Lifestyle issues such as work schedule, commute time, and opportunity for social activities.

- Compensation (e.g., salary, overtime pay, and performance bonus) and benefits (e.g., retirement plan options, medical plan options, dental plan, eye care plan, disability insurance, liability insurance, long-term care insurance, tuition waiver plan, flexible spending account, child care, stock options, vacation, holiday time, and sick leave).

If you receive several offers that interest you, conduct a thorough evaluation of personal considerations. To compare offers simultaneously, prepare a chart similar to the one in Table 9.1 below, which shows an evaluation of three hypothetical positions. Consider weighting areas of importance to determine a final score.

Table 9.1 Criteria for Evaluating Position Offers

Directions: Determine the level of importance of each criterion by assigning a weighting factor expressed as a percentage of the total. Use the scale below to assign a rating for each criterion pertaining to each position.

Rating Scale: Unacceptable   1   2   3   4   5   6   7   8   9   10   Ideal

Criteria	Weighting Factor (%)	Position A		Position B		Position C	
		Rating (1-10)	Total Score (Weight x Rate)	Rating (1-10)	Total Score (Weight x Rate)	Rating (1-10)	Total Score (Weight x Rate)
Position (match of knowledge, skills, attitudes)	30%	6	1.8	7	2.1	4	1.2
Organization (size, management structure, reputation, opportunities for advancement, work environment)	30%	8	2.4	9	2.7	8	2.4
Geographic Location (cost of living, housing availability, climate)	10%	3	0.3	6	0.6	5	0.5
Life Style Issues (schedule, commute time, social activities)	15%	5	0.8	4	0.6	7	1.1
Compensation (salary, benefits)	15%	5	0.8	8	1.2	9	1.4
TOTAL	100%		6.1		7.2		6.6

Chapter 10

Interview Questions

Your ability to answer questions clearly and thoughtfully represents an important part of any interview. Most interviewers rely on a series of questions to determine your suitability for a specific position. They will probably ask some questions related to the organization and the opportunity you seek. Other generic questions will probe your background, communication skills, and personal style.

In this chapter, you will find common questions you may encounter during an interview session. During any given session, interviewers can only ask a fraction of these questions—but this list will help you brainstorm suitable responses.

Take time to think about these questions. You may think you know your life history by heart, but details fade, and without careful reflection, people don't always recognize their own accomplishments. Do not plan out meticulous answers to each question. Focus on questions most closely related to your qualifications and the type of position you seek. You can jot down thoughts and rehearse answers, but do not memorize your responses.

In all your responses, be brief—no more than 90 to 120 seconds, or a maximum of roughly 350 words. Use positive words and phrases, even when you are discussing difficult topics such as why you left a previous position. (For example, "I am seeking more challenges," not "I didn't have enough responsibility" or "My boss was a jerk.") Keep your responses focused and give concrete examples of your successes.

This chapter contains several categories of questions. For each category, consider the special points noted as you contemplate possible answers.

Accomplishments

Although your résumé or CV may clearly identify your personal and professional accomplishments, you will usually get an opportunity during the interview session to discuss them. Routine questions such as "Tell me about your most satisfying accomplishment in life" or "What do you consider your most important idea or suggestion that your current employer implemented?" allow you to focus on one or more of your important accomplishments. In these situations, stay focused on your professional accomplishments. Try to discuss recent ones, since they are fresher in your mind and you will have a better chance of providing specific details. Always include a brief discussion of your accomplishments when you respond to the question "Tell me about yourself." Possible accomplishment questions include:

> Always include a brief discussion of your accomplishments when you respond to the question, "Tell me about yourself."

- What do you consider to be your most important idea or suggestion that your current employer implemented?

- Tell me about an award or recognition certificate you have received.

- Tell me about your most satisfying accomplishment in life.

- Tell me about your most satisfying accomplishment as a pharmacist [pharmacy student, technician].

- Tell me how you supported your present or past employer in reaching a departmental goal.

- Tell me about a quantifiable outcome from one of your efforts at work.

- Describe a technical skill you developed and perfected during the past year.

- Describe an improvement in your current work setting that you personally initiated.

- How do you measure your success at work?

- How do you handle success?

- Tell me about a time when you completed an assignment that was well received by your employer.

- Tell me which one of your publications gave you the greatest personal satisfaction and why.

- What do you consider the most significant accomplishment in your professional career?

- What achievement at work has given you the greatest sense of personal accomplishment?

- Tell me about a time when your idea or action reduced an expense for your employer.

- Tell me your five most significant accomplishments at your current place of employment. Why do you think your employer considers them important?

- What academic honors or awards did you receive in college?

Career Development

Interviewers like to compare your goals and objectives with those of their organization or program. The career goal statement listed in your résumé or curriculum vitae offers a great opening for the discussion. Keep in mind that short-term goals span one or two years, while long-term goals extend three to five years ahead.

Review the organization's goals in advance to ensure compatibility with yours. Most likely, you will want a position that gives you the chance to acquire new knowledge and skills so you can advance within the profession or assume additional responsibilities. Possible career development questions include:

- What career goals have you set for the future? Have these changed since you graduated?

- How has your career progressed in relation to your career plan?

- What would you like to accomplish during the next five years?

- How do your current career goals differ from the career goals you set five years ago?

- Where do you see yourself in the next five years?

- Have you ever considered leaving the profession of pharmacy? If so, what career choice would you select?

- Tell me why you think this is the right position for you at this point in your career.

- What career plans do you have beyond this position?

- What other career opportunities would you like to experience?

- Which of the career tracks offered by our company do you find most appealing?

- Have you ever considered taking a position that was not part of your career plan?

- If you could begin your career path again, what changes would you make?

- In climbing a career ladder, how critical is it for you to reach the top rung?

- Why have you considered changing your career path in pharmacy at this point in your life?

- Would you like to have your current supervisor's position?

- How much thought do you give to your future?

- To what extent does this position fit with your overall career plan? Does it present inconsistencies with your plan?

- How do you feel about the progress of your career to date?

- Describe the ideal position based on your long-term career plan.

- What would you change if you were graduating from high school today and planning your career path?

- What are your short-term (one- to two-year) career goals? How do you plan to achieve them?

- What are your long-term (three- to five-year) career goals? How do you plan to achieve them?

- How do you determine if your career plan is on track?

- What made you choose pharmacy as a career?

- How do you see your career changing over the next few years? What are you doing to prepare yourself for these changes?

- Your résumé lacks any documentation of employment during the past four years. Why?

- I noticed that you have not worked for several years. What have you done to keep up with changes in the profession?

- Tell me about the interruptions in your employment history.

- Who had the greatest influence on your choice of pharmacy as a career path?

- Describe a major career planning goal that you recently established for yourself. How do you plan to achieve this goal?

Coping with Change

The health care industry involves constant change, and successful employees must learn to adapt. The changes discussed in the interview process often focus on technology, human resources, administrative leadership, or professional services. Prepare yourself to share one or more examples of significant change in your present work setting and how you adjusted. Some examples of these questions include:

- How do you handle change at work?

- Describe a time you had to change your leadership [management] style.

- Do you prefer a structured routine in your daily work or frequent change?

- Change has contributed to our department's success during the past few years. Tell me about your ability to deal with change.

- Describe a time when a change at work had a significant impact on your work or responsibilities. How did you adjust?

- Tell me about a time when you were involved in a project or assignment at work that resulted in a significant positive [negative] change.

- How do you deal with individuals who resist change?

- Tell me about a time when change led to downsizing in your organization. How did you deal with the situation?

Communication Skills

Pharmacy professionals need strong written and verbal communication skills. Your résumé, curriculum vitae, and cover letters provide key vehicles for demonstrating your writing skills. Interviewers will assess your speaking ability—how clearly and in what manner you convey information—during the interview session. Possible communication-related questions include:

- How do you routinely communicate with your subordinates [superiors]?

- How would you rate your writing abilities?

- How would you rate your oral presentation skills?

- What process do you follow in preparing a presentation?

- How do you "stay connected" with your colleagues?

- Describe your experience in making oral presentations.

- Tell me about a quality presentation you delivered. What made it successful?

- How would you compare your oral presentation skills to your writing skills?

- Have you ever experienced writer's block? How did you overcome this?

- Do you prefer to write or speak? Why?

- Tell me about your most difficult writing assignment. What did you learn?

- How would you describe your listening skills?

- What approach have you used to improve your mastery of English as a spoken language?

- What is your greatest challenge in responding to electronic messages?

Dealing with Conflict

Conflict exists in any work setting. Interviewers who want to determine your ability to cope with conflict will probably ask situation-based questions such as "Tell me about a time you had to deal with an irate patient. How did you handle the situation?" Most people, even those with modest work experience, can usually discuss one or more incidents involving conflict. Think about past examples with a positive outcome and relate a story that demonstrates your ability to deal with conflict. Possible conflict-related questions include:

> Most people, even those with modest work experience, can usually discuss one or more incidents involving conflict.

- Do you prefer to confront conflict or tactfully avoid it?

- How do you go about confronting your colleagues when problems occur?

- How do you attempt to avoid conflict?

- Do you prefer to address small issues before they become problems or wait to see if they resolve on their own?

- Have you ever lost your temper at work?

- How do you handle conflict?

- How do you deal with your colleagues after a difficult situation has been resolved?

- Tell me about a time when you had to deal with an irate patient [physician, nurse, student]. How did you handle the situation?

- Tell me about a situation where you avoided siding with a colleague about a difficult issue.

- Tell me about a time when you needed to work closely with someone you routinely disagree with. How did you deal with the situation?

- Describe a time when you successfully resolved a conflict between two of your colleagues.

- How do you deal with "office politics?"

- Tell me about a situation where you had a personal commitment that resulted in a conflict with your work schedule. What did you do?

- Describe a time when you did not successfully resolve a conflict with one of your colleagues.

- Describe a time when you successfully resolved a conflict with one of your colleagues.

Creativity

Employers like to see evidence that employees can be inventive and think "outside the box." Make sure you can present examples from your past work experiences that demonstrate your ability to think creatively in the work setting. Some examples of these questions include:

- Tell me about a time while not at work that you got an idea that helped you become more successful at work.

- If you were planning a trip to the moon and could only take three things, what would you take?

- If you were a drug, what drug would you be? Why?

- Convince me that I need to buy the chair you are sitting in.

- What would you do if this was your last week on earth?

> Make sure you can present examples from your past work experiences that demonstrate your ability to think creatively in the work setting.

- How would you like people to remember you?

- Describe your most innovative work assignment.

- Describe a time when your personal creativity helped solve a problem at work.

- Tell me about a time when you improved something that was already working fine.

- Tell me about your participation in a really creative project.

- What areas of research interest you?

- Describe something creative you have done as an employee [student].

- If you were hospitalized, who would you like to share your semi-private room with?

Handling Criticism

Dealing with criticism constructively represents an important element of self-assessment and self-improvement. When an interviewer asks how you handle criticism, describe an incident that demonstrates what you learned from the critical comments of a supervisor or coworker. Possible questions include:

- Tell me about a time when you were unfairly criticized. How did you handle the situation?

- What is your approach for dealing with constructive criticism?

- If your supervisor was unfair in his or her criticism of your work performance, what would you do?

When an interviewer asks how you handle criticism, describe an incident that demonstrates what you learned from the critical comments of a supervisor or coworker.

- Describe a situation where your work was justifiably criticized.

- What would you do if I said that I thought your interview skills were less than I expect for an individual with your experience?

- Has one of your professors ever assigned a grade lower than you deserved? If so, what did you do?

Decision-Making Skills

Decision-making figures prominently into professional success. Interviewers may ask about the types of decisions you have difficultly making and how you make decisions in the absence of adequate data. Relate recent examples that demonstrate your ability to make decisions—especially examples related to situations likely to occur in the position you seek. Common decision-making questions include:

- What kind of decisions do you find most difficult to make?

- On her way to a three-day business meeting, your supervisor leaves an assignment with incomplete and unclear instructions. You have no luck in reaching her. How would you handle this situation?

Relate recent examples that demonstrate your ability to make decisions—especially examples related to situations likely to occur in the position you seek.

- Your supervisor directs you to complete an assignment with incorrect instructions. How would you handle this situation?

- What approach do you use to make important decisions?

- How did you handle the most difficult decision you ever had to make?

- After you make a decision, do you ever change your mind?

- To what extent does intuition play an important part of your decision-making process?

- Tell me about a time when you made an unpopular decision. How did you handle this situation?

- Describe a situation when you had to make a quick decision without the ability to gather all the facts.

- Have you ever made a decision without the knowledge of a standard operating procedure to assist you?

- Give me some examples of decisions that you routinely make in your current position. How do you go about making these decisions?

- Tell me about a time when you had to defend your decision.

- Which types of decisions do you find easy [difficult] to make? Why?

- Think about an important decision that you made in the past. Would you make the same decision today? Why or why not?

- To what extent do you seek information from others before making a decision?

- How have your decision-making skills improved in the last few years? What factors have contributed to this improvement?

Educational Experience

Although interviewers can learn much about your educational experience from your résumé or curriculum vitae, they will probably want to know more about its depth and breadth and how it relates to the position you seek—especially if you recently graduated. Stay focused on your academic strengths and avoid concentrating on weaker academic performance in a specific course. If they consider grades a critical determinant for employment, interviewers will probably have reviewed your academic transcript in advance. No matter what kind of student you were, discuss ways you've successfully applied your knowledge in the work setting. Possible education-related questions include:

- Does your overall grade point average on your college transcript adequately reflect your academic ability?

- How do you think your academic performance will correlate with your work performance?

- Where did you rank in your graduating class in high school [college, pharmacy school]?

- How did you choose the college or university you attended?

- What subjects did you enjoy most [least] in pharmacy school?

- If you had it to do over again, what changes would you make as a pharmacy [college, high school] student?

- If you were entering a pharmacy degree program again, which courses would you devote more time to fully understand?

- In what courses did you earn low [high] grades? How do you think that will affect your work performance?

- What were a few of your most [least] favorite college courses? Why?

- Which year of college was the most difficult for you? Why?

- On average, how many hours do you estimate that you spent studying per week when you were earning your pharmacy degree?

- Did you work full-time or part-time while earning your pharmacy degree?

- How did you pay for your college education?

- What aspects of your pharmacy [college, high school] education did you enjoy most?

- Tell me more about the factors that led you to select the topic for your thesis.

- What are the major findings of your thesis?

- What process did you follow to select your thesis advisor?

- What was the role of your thesis advisor in guiding the completion of your work?

- What publications have resulted from your graduate work?

- How did you pay for your graduate education?

- How well do you think academic performance correlates with productivity as an employee?

Issues Related to the Employer or Position

Become as familiar as you can with the position description and the organization so you can adeptly handle questions related to the employer and position. Prepare a list of your ideal job or position preferences, such as location, type of practice setting, level of supervision desired, characteristics of ideal colleagues, and work schedule. Also, reflect on your past performance evaluations and prepare to describe the strengths they identified. If asked to talk about your weaknesses, do not spill out every flaw you think you have. Simply identify an area that you improved and explain the positive changes that resulted. Position-related questions may include:

- What work conditions allow you to perform most successfully in activities you undertake?

- Why do you want this position?

- Describe your ideal work environment.

- What do you find most [least] appealing about this position? Why?

- What do you think about customer service?

- Tell me about a current responsibility that you enjoy as an employee.

- Thinking about your past supervisors, who did you like the most? What were the traits that you liked about this individual?

- Thinking about your past supervisors, who did you like the least? Why? What, if anything, could you have done to improve the relationship?

- If you could change one thing about your most recent employer, what would you change?

- How would your most recent supervisor describe your work habits?

> If asked to talk about your weaknesses, do not spill out every flaw you think you have. Simply identify an area that you improved and explain the positive changes that resulted.

- What do you perceive as differences between this position and your most recent position?

- Tell me about your relationship with your previous supervisors.

- Do you perceive your current or most recent employer as being sensitive to employee needs? Do you think this organization will act differently?

- I see that you have held various jobs. Which one did you like most? Why?

- I see that you have held many jobs for short periods of time. How long would you plan to stay here?

- I see that you have stayed with one employer for a long time. Does this reflect a sense of loyalty or a lack of initiative?

- Why do you want to leave your current position?

- Describe your best [worst] supervisor.

- What have your past supervisors identified as your strengths [weaknesses]?

- Describe a typical work day in your most recent position.

- Tell me about a situation at work when you exceeded your supervisor's expectations.

- Would you recommend your most recent employer to your friends? Why or why not?

- Have you ever resigned from a position with less than two weeks' notice? If so, what were the circumstances?

- Have any of your past employers ever refused to give you a reference? If so, what were the circumstances?

- Does your current employer know about this interview today?

- Have you ever been terminated? If so, what were the circumstances?

- Have you ever been asked to resign? If so, what were the circumstances?

- What kind of supervisors motivate you to do your best work?

- How would you describe your current supervisor's management style? Which aspects do you like the most [least]? Why?

- How would you describe your relationship with your current supervisor?

- What do you like most [least] about your current position?

- What do you want to achieve in your next position?

- How do you feel about the contributions you made to your most recent employer?

- What has been the pattern of your relationships with supervisors or upper management?

- What would you plan to achieve in this position that you did not achieve in your most recent position?

- What limitations exist in your current position?

- In your most recent position, how much time did you spend working by yourself? Working with others? Do you ever work as a member of a team to complete projects or other assignments?

- In your most recent position, how often did you meet with your supervisor? What was the nature of these meetings?

- Tell me about your last three positions (your major responsibilities, description of the work environment, the relationship with your supervisor and coworkers).

- In your current position, how much time during a typical day do you devote to communications (telephone calls, meetings, presentations, correspondence)?

- If you decide to stay with your current employer, what expectations do you have concerning advancement?

- If you like your current employer and position, why do you plan to leave?

- Since you have expressed difficulties with your current supervisor, what have you done to bring these problems to his or her attention?

- What have you learned from past supervisors?

- How would you characterize the workload associated with your most recent position?

- To what extent has your most recent position prepared you to assume additional responsibilities and duties?

- In your most recent position, how many levels of management existed between your position and the chief executive officer?

- Describe your relationship and dealings with upper management.

- In your most recent position, what changes did you initiate to enhance the efficiency of the organization?

- Tell me about a situation in your most recent position that you never want to experience again.

- Tell me about a time when your most recent supervisor was not pleased with your job performance.

- Have you ever been denied an opportunity for advancement that you felt you deserved? How did you handle the situation?

- What kind of employee rewards do you like?

- Tell me about a time when you may have expected too much from your employer. How did you handle the situation?

- What skills do you think you need most for success in this position?

- If we hire you into this position, what skills would you like to develop?

- If you decide to stay in your current position, how could you improve the position?

- What strengths did you bring to your most recent position that contributed to your success?

- What strengths will make you successful in this position?

- Of the various settings you have worked in, which environment caused you to be the most [least] productive?

- How would you compare your past three positions with what you like?

- What specific knowledge and skills do you need to improve for successful performance in this position? What can you do to overcome these possible deficiencies?

- How would you rate your potential success in this position? Why?

- What responsibilities in your most recent position did you find difficult to fulfill?

- Can you work overtime shifts, if needed?

- What would you have liked to achieve in your most recent position that was beyond your reach?

- What qualifications do you think you need for this position and how can you satisfy them?

- Tell me what you know about our organization. How did you obtain this information?

- What particular aspects of this organization appear most interesting to you?

- Give me your impression of our company within the marketplace.

- Where do you think we are the most vulnerable as an industry?

- From your perspective, describe our company's primary competition.

- What would you do if a competitor offered you a position similar to the one discussed here?

- How actively have you searched for a position?

- What trends do you see in our industry?

- If you were in my position, what type of experience would you consider important for this position?

- What do you see in common between this position and your most recent position?

- What differences do you see between this position and your most recent position?

- How did you learn about this open position?

- During the past six months, have you arrived late to work? How often, and what were the circumstances?

- What have you heard about our organization that raises concerns in your mind?

- How will you handle the least appealing aspects of this position?

- What aspects of this position can you confidently fulfill?

- What aspects of this position raise concerns about your abilities?

- In three minutes or less, tell me why we should hire you [why you are the best candidate for this position].

- What do you think about our facilities and operations?

- What process did you use to select your references?

- How long will it take for you to contribute to our organization's success?

- After reviewing your résumé, most reasonable managers might conclude that you have too much experience for this position. What do you think?

- After reviewing your résumé, it appears that you lack the requisite qualifications for this position. Why should I hire you?

- What characteristics do you want most in a position?

- Based on what you have learned about our organization and this position, what additional factors should we consider in hiring someone?

- A number of applicants are being interviewed for this position. Why should we consider you for the position?

- Did you consider yourself to have a sense of loyalty to any of your past employers? Why or why not?

- Name one particular characteristic or skill that should make you more successful than other candidates for this position.

- Often, employees are either concept-oriented or task-oriented. How would you describe yourself?

- Do you enjoy routine tasks and duties at work?

Knowledge of Issues Facing the Profession

Keeping up to date on issues facing the profession remains essential—especially matters that may have a key bearing on the position you seek. Interviewers will probably want you to discuss current issues, including controversial ones within the profession. Possible questions in this area include:

- What recommendations can you suggest to improve safe medication practices?

- In your opinion, should the profession support a mandatory reporting system for serious or fatal adverse events?

- What does the term "pharmaceutical care" mean to you?

- How do you see the role of the pharmacist changing in the next five years?

- What recommendations would you suggest to support public and private insurance payment to pharmacists for patient services that improve clinical and economic outcomes?

- In your opinion, do pharmacists need credentialing to participate in disease state management programs?

- How would you try to initiate a collaborative practice agreement with a physician?

- What clinical evidence exists to support the value of pharmacists in providing patient care services?

- What role does direct-to-consumer advertising play in educating patients about prescription medications?

- What major challenges do you think the profession will face over the next 10 years?

- Describe opportunities for initiating a pharmaceutical care practice.

- What measures can pharmacists take to reduce the incidence of medication errors?

- What impact will telemedicine technology have on the practice of pharmacy?

- Should the general public have access to data from clinical drug trials?

- Who should bear responsibility for certifying pharmacists to participate in disease state management activities?

- Which cognitive services provided by pharmacists result in a positive cost benefit to patients and payers?

- Why have pharmacists been ranked as one of the most respected health professionals during the past decade?

- How would you advise a patient to choose his or her personal pharmacist?

- What role should pharmacists play in response to a disaster such as an influenza pandemic?

- How can technology enhance the role of the practicing pharmacist?

- What single greatest challenge does the profession face in the next two years?

- What important trends do you see in our profession?

- What do you feel it takes to be a professional?

- What does the term "professionalism" mean to you?

- Describe an ethical dilemma you faced in a practice situation. How did you deal with it?

Leadership Qualities

Although they relate directly to people seeking administrative responsibilities, questions about leadership qualities may apply to any position within the profession. Most interviewers will want to determine your ability to serve as a role model for others. When responding, try to use the term "we" rather than "I" to suggest that you value and make the most of teamwork. Leadership-related questions may include:

> Most interviewers will want to determine your ability to serve as a role model for others.

- What leadership positions, if any, did you hold in pharmacy student organizations? How were you selected for these positions?

- Tell me about a time when you persuaded others to accept your recommendation or advice.

- How would a coworker describe your leadership style?

- Describe the characteristics of a leader you admire.

- Tell me about a time when you led a project with a positive [negative] outcome.

- What kept you from greater participation in extracurricular activities when you were in pharmacy school [college, high school]?

- How do you go about influencing someone to accept your ideas?

- Tell me about your commitment to maintaining a diverse work force.

- Give me examples of how you have demonstrated leadership qualities in your current position.

- Who is your favorite leader in pharmacy? Why?

- Tell me about an effective leader you have known. In your opinion, what made this individual effective?

Commitment to Life-Long Learning

Because knowledge in the health care community expands so rapidly, you must commit yourself to continual learning. Pharmacy school provides a great foundation, but learning actually begins with graduation. At interviews, discuss your continuing education programs, professional meetings, certificate programs, or other types of learning programs. Questions interviewers may ask you include:

- Describe your three most significant learning experiences during the past six months.

- Do you plan to pursue additional studies?

- How much time do you spend each month keeping up with the professional literature? Which professional journals do you routinely read?

- Do you currently take, or do you plan to take, evening courses?

- Do you subscribe to any professional journals? Which ones?

- In the last year, have you attended any pharmacy continuing education programs?

- How do you keep up with the scientific advances in drug therapy?

Management Skills and Abilities

When you apply for a supervisory position you will get asked questions related to management abilities. These questions probe specific skills such as planning, organizing, directing, and controlling. Review the duties you carried out in your past positions to help you give specific examples. Possible questions include:

> Management-related questions probe specific skills such as planning, organizing, directing, and controlling.

- Have you overseen budgeting, approved expenses, and monitored departmental progress against financial goals? How qualified do you feel in performing these activities?

- Tell me about your supervision of other individuals in your past positions.

- Tell me about a learning experience that affected your management style.

- Give me examples of what you did in your most recent position to increase revenues and reduce costs.

- Have you ever had to hire people? For what types of positions?

- What characteristics do you look for in individuals you plan to hire?

- Have you ever fired anyone? What were the circumstances?

- What type of management style do you think proves effective in managing health professionals?

- Describe your management style. What aspects would you like to change? Why?

- Tell me about a time when you did not receive full support in the completion of a task and how you dealt with it.

- Are you an effective manager? Give me examples of your management effectiveness.

- Tell me about the people you hired in your current job. How long did they stay with you? How did their coworkers view them?

- What process would you use to address an employee with an unsatisfactory performance evaluation?

- How do you identify deficiencies in your subordinates?

- Give examples of your ability to delegate.

- Tell me about a time when you dealt with an employee displaying inappropriate behavior in your work setting.

- What characteristics does an effective department director display?

- How would you describe your management philosophy?

- Give me examples of how you balance autonomy and control among your employees.

- How do you effectively evaluate the performance of your staff?

- How would your staff describe your management style?

- What techniques have you found effective for motivating your staff?

- Tell me about one of your former employees who was promoted as a result of your mentoring.

- How do you prefer to recognize and reward your staff for excellent work performance?

- How do you train and develop your staff?

- How do you differentiate between management and leadership?

- Would you describe yourself as a manager or a leader? Can you elaborate?

- Give me examples of your ability to manage resources effectively.

- Tell me about a time when you negotiated a conflict between two of your most [least] successful employees.

- What strengths [weaknesses] do you display as a manager?

- If you left your current position, do you have someone to take your place? How have you developed this person to assume your responsibilities?

- Give examples of how you enhanced the effectiveness of your immediate superior in your most recent position.

- Tell me about your experience in dealing with external consultants. How did you use their recommendations for improving your department?

- Tell me about a time when you made a bad hiring decision.

- What process have you found useful in planning?

- How do you go about organizing and planning for the successful completion of a major project or event?

- Give me examples of how you handle multiple projects or assignments.

- What process did you use to prepare for this interview?

- Tell me about a time when you became sidetracked with the details of an assignment.

- How would you describe your attitude toward taking risks?

- How do you respond to the concept of "no risk, no reward?"

- What risks did you take in your most recent position? What results did taking these risks achieve?

- Do you consider yourself a risk taker? Give me examples of risks you have taken in previous positions.

- Tell me about an experience at work where the risks outweighed the rewards. How did you deal with this situation?

- How did you go about obtaining your most recent position?

Maintaining Peer Relationships

Pharmacy professionals must work as a team, not only within the profession, but with members of the other health disciplines. Employers and program directors want to know that you have the right interpersonal skills for building and maintaining positive relationships. Interviewers will observe how well you relate to others and want to hear current examples of your skills, especially how you deal with "difficult" personality styles. Possible peer relationship questions include:

> Interviewers will observe how well you relate to others and want to hear current examples of your skills.

- Describe your working relationship with peers.

- When assigned to a team, what types of coworkers do you like most as teammates?

- How would you describe your coworkers at your most recent place of employment?

- How do you deal with weaknesses in others?

- What do you consider the ideal mix of individuals for a productive work team?

- How would you compare the quality and quantity of your work to that of your coworkers?

- Do you prefer working alone or with others?

- In your most recent position, how did you relate to coworkers with more [fewer] years of experience?

- How do you like to work with other people when completing projects?

- Tell me about your ability to get along with classmates [faculty members, coworkers].

- What types of people irritate you at work?

- Tell me about the types of people you like to associate with at work.

- Do you enjoy meeting people?

- Tell me about a time when you were not successful in getting along with a coworker. How did you resolve the issue?

Personal Attributes

Most of us do not normally recite a litany of our personal strengths, but in an interview you must do just that. Emphasize attributes such as exhibiting a strong work ethic and being self-motivated, enthusiastic, loyal, a team player, dependable, flexible, and caring. When discussing attributes, tie their relevance to the position you seek. Possible personal attribute questions include:

- What personal characteristics do you consider ideal for a pharmacist? How do these match your personal characteristics? How do they differ?

- What makes you different from other pharmacists [technicians, students, employees]?

- How do you measure personal success?

- Give me examples of your determination.

- Tell me about a time when your persistence paid off at work.

- How do I know you are a sincere person?

- How hard have you worked to achieve your career goals?

- Tell me about a time when you were right, but others disagreed. How did you deal with the situation?

- Tell me about a time when you accomplished a task that required a significant amount of discipline.

- In your most recent position, did you work harder than your coworkers?

- What motivates you to excel?

- List five things that motivate you to do your best work.

- Are you self-motivated? Give me examples of how you display initiative at work.

> Emphasize attributes such as exhibiting a strong work ethic and being self-motivated, enthusiastic, loyal, a team player, dependable, flexible, and caring.

- How do you motivate other people?

- How has competition affected your achievements? Give me examples of positive [negative] impacts.

- Which has greater value to you, a large salary or recognition and career advancement?

- What personal rewards do you want from your job?

- Tell me about a long-standing interest or activity of yours.

- How do you unwind in your spare time?

- What percent of your college expenses did you earn? How?

- What did you do during your summers while you were in college?

- How do you balance your outside activities with your work?

- Do you stick to a schedule on your days away from work?

- Tell me about a movie that inspired you.

- I did not see any hobbies or outside activities listed on your résumé. What do you like to do in your time away from work?

- Do you enjoy reading? What is your favorite book [magazine]?

- Tell me about the last book you read.

- How would your best friend [college roommate, favorite supervisor, coworkers] describe you?

- If you could change one thing about your personality, what would it be? Why?

- How do you like to spend your time relaxing when not at work?

- What section of the daily newspaper do you like most?

- What television program do you like most?

- Do you include coworkers in your social life?

- Tell me about an interesting trip you have taken.

- How would you describe your personality?

- What importance do you place on being liked by your colleagues?

- Who do you consider your best friend? Why is this individual special to you?

- Tell me something about yourself that you have not included in your résumé.

- Will you relocate, if necessary?

- What will you do if we do not offer this position to you?

- How do you feel about having a dress code in a work environment made up of health professionals?

- Tell me about yourself.

- If I could remember only one thing about you, what should it be?

- How do you feel about being tested for drug use?

- How do you explain your career success?

- Tell me about a time when you exceeded the expectations of your supervisor.

- What sites do you routinely visit on the World Wide Web?

Problem-Solving Skills

Pharmacy professionals face many problems on a daily basis. Interviewers will want to determine your ability to think problems through, apply knowledge, and develop effective solutions. Problem-solving questions may include:

- Tell me about a recurring work problem that you resolved.

- Give me examples of major projects you have completed.

- Tell me about a time when you were assigned to complete an unpopular task.

- How do you usually approach solving problems?

- Where do you turn when your usual problem-solving approaches do not work?

- Give me examples of how you have successfully used problem-solving techniques.

- Tell me about the most difficult problem you ever confronted.

- Give me an example of a problem that was not resolved to your satisfaction.

> Interviewers will want to determine your ability to think problems through, apply knowledge, and develop effective solutions.

- How do you approach problems or difficult assignments that you would prefer to avoid?

- Describe a situation where you were not successful in resolving a problem. How did you finally deal with this situation?

- Tell me about a time when you were asked to solve a problem without sufficient resources. How did you resolve the problem?

- If you encounter an unsatisfied patient, what do you typically do?

- Tell me about a time when you used a creative approach to solve a difficult problem.

- Tell me about a time when you overlooked a simple solution to solve a problem.

Professional and Other Employment Experience

Experiential learning allows you to apply a wide range of knowledge and skills. In describing your past positions, highlight the skills you developed and the aspects of your work that you liked. You can also touch upon the aspects you disliked—without going overboard or sounding too negative. It helps to prepare a list of the characteristics you associate with the ideal work setting. Questions may include:

- What do you consider the most important thing you have learned from your most recent position?

- How will your military experience assist you with the responsibilities of this position?

- As a recent graduate, how will you compensate for your lack of experience in this position?

- Do you believe your qualifications [professional experiences] will enable you to become successful in this position?

- How does your current position relate to the mission and goals of the organization?

- How do you rate your clinical knowledge and skills?

- How do you rate your past experience in relation to the responsibilities of this position?

- I see that you have held a variety of positions. Overall, what have you learned from your work experience?

- Which of your clerkship experiences was the most [least] professionally satisfying? Why?

- What would your pharmacy preceptors tell me about your ability to apply knowledge in a practice setting?

- Tell me about your experience in preparing and compounding intravenous admixture preparations.

- Give me examples of recommendations you have made to physicians about medication treatment plans that reduced the risk of patient harm.

- Tell me about the outcome of a clinical intervention that you made within the past two months.

- Tell me about your experience in promoting rational drug therapy based on the use of a formulary.

- What approach do you use to document the impact of your patient interventions?

- Give me examples of your interactions with other health care providers in caring for patients.

- During the last year, have you participated in any health care promotion activities? What were the impacts?

- Give me examples of your participation in the activities of local, state, or national pharmacy organizations.

- What makes you an effective teacher?

- Tell me about your experiences in precepting pharmacy students in the practice setting.

- Your résumé indicates that you've been working as a part-time pharmacy technician. How will this experience help you achieve your career goals?

Salary Issues

Ideally, you will not have to talk about salary until you receive a job offer. If salary-related questions come up in the interview, you can answer them in a positive way without stating your actual salary expectations. For example, you might say that you have an idea of the market, but for the moment you would like to hear more about the position. Or you might say that you find it difficult to formulate salary expectations without knowing the complete benefits package and the nature of the work environment. If you filled out an application form you may already have provided your current salary, so make sure you quote the same amount to the interviewer, if asked. When discussing salary, remember to focus on the total compensation package and not merely the pay. Possible salary-related questions include:

> If salary-related questions come up in the interview, you can answer them in a positive way without stating your actual salary expectations.

- What would you like to earn five years from now?

- Do you believe your current salary reflects your experience and performance evaluations?

- How do you feel about a reduction in salary from your most recent position?

- How much do you value job security?

- Tell me about your salary expectations.

- Have you ever been denied a salary increase? What were the circumstances?

- What do you currently earn?

- What do you expect for a compensation package?

Dealing with Self-Assessment

Everyone has strengths and weaknesses, but when asked "self-assessment" questions, people commonly focus more on the areas where they need improvement. When discussing deficiencies, emphasize your awareness of the problem and your actions for improvement. Likewise, identify one or two strengths and describe how they positively impact the position you seek. Self-assessment questions may include:

- If you could change one thing about yourself, what would you change? Why?

- What adjectives would you use to describe yourself?

- What do you consider your biggest strengths [weaknesses]?

- How does your personality manifest itself when you deal with stressful situations at work?

- Tell me about a time when you failed. How did you handle the situation?

- Do you consider yourself successful? Why?

- To what degree were you satisfied with your performance in your most recent position?

- How would you describe yourself when you were in college? How have you changed since graduating?

- What experience do you need most to advance your career?

- What do you consider the greatest disappointment in your career, to date? How did you overcome this?

> When discussing deficiencies, emphasize your awareness of the problem and your actions for improvement. Likewise, identify one or two strengths and describe how they positively impact the position you seek.

- How would you characterize the quality and quantity of your work in your past positions?

- What have you learned from your mistakes?

- How do you reconcile any differences between reality and your expectations?

- What tasks or duties do you find difficult? What have you done to overcome these difficulties?

- How would you rank yourself among your peers?

- Tell me about a time at work when you were disappointed with your performance.

- Have you ever been called on by one of your professors when you were unsure about the answer? How did you respond?

- What do you consider the most intellectually challenging activity you have ever performed?

- How important do you consider details?

- What plan do you have for improving your professional qualifications?

- Have you considered pursuing an advanced degree?

- What plan do you have for improving your knowledge and skills?

- What work habits have you sought to improve?

- During the past three years, what have you done to improve your professional knowledge and skills?

Stress Management

If managed properly, stress can positively impact a situation. Make sure you can discuss your approaches for coping with stress. Also, provide examples of working under pressure, especially those with positive outcomes. Possible stress management questions include:

- How do you respond to deadlines?

- Tell me about your ability to work under pressure.

- How do you manage stress in your daily work?

- How do you handle stressful situations with your supervisor [coworkers]?

- Tell me about a time when you worked under significant pressure to meet a deadline.

- What measures do you take to avoid burnout?

Teamwork

People rarely work in isolation. Teamwork applies in just about every work environment, especially in pharmacy practice settings. Recall one or more experiences you had as a team member at work and describe your contribution to the team. Possible teamwork questions may include:

- How do you feel as a team member when your project isn't successful? How do you deal with the situation?

- How do you promote "esprit de corps" among members of a team at work?

- Do you consider yourself a team player?

- Describe a situation when the team fell apart. What was your role in the outcome?

- Tell me about a time when you were effective in convincing team members to adopt your recommendation.

- Tell me about a contribution you made as a member of a team at work.

- Tell me about a time when you increased your productivity by serving as a team member at work.

- What type of role do you generally assume when assigned to a team?

- Tell me about a time when you learned about teamwork through your participation in a sport.

- What quality do you value the most in a team member?

Technical Knowledge and Skills

Some employers may want to examine your technical knowledge, assess your skills at applying it, and gauge your ability to "think on your feet." To do this, they might have you review a scenario commonly associated with the position you seek. For example, they might ask a pharmacist seeking a clinical specialist position to review a patient case and develop an optimal drug treatment plan. Questions employers may ask include:

- Describe your familiarity with computer systems and software applications.

- What is the latest computer software application that you have learned?

- Review the following case of a patient with [a common chronic or acute disease] and outline a plan for drug therapy management.

- Review the following case of a patient with [a common chronic or acute disease] and [any other common chronic or acute disease]. Outline a plan for drug therapy management.

- Review the following case describing a common drug interaction [adverse drug reaction]. How would you resolve the problem?

- Review the following case describing a patient with a history of medication non-compliance. Design a plan to improve the patient's medication taking behavior.

> Some employers may want to examine your technical knowledge, assess your skills at applying it, and gauge your ability to "think on your feet."

- Review the following case of a patient with diabetes [seizure disorder, high blood pressure, lipid disorder, congestive heart failure, tuberculosis, bipolar disease, urinary tract infection, Parkinson's disease] and outline a plan for drug therapy management.

- Review the following case of a patient with bronchitis and a history of anxiety. Outline a plan for drug therapy management.

- Review the following case of a patient with asthma and contact dermatitis. Outline a plan for drug therapy management.

- Review the following case of a patient with rheumatoid arthritis and a duodenal ulcer. Outline a plan for drug therapy management.

- Review the following case of a patient with angina pectoris and deep vein thrombosis. Outline a plan for drug therapy management.

- Review the following case of a patient with bacterial pneumonia and congestive heart failure. Outline a plan for drug therapy management.

- Review the following case of a patient with atrial fibrillation and a history of migraine headaches. Outline a plan for drug therapy management.

- Review the following case of a patient with chronic depression and symptoms of the common cold. Outline a plan for drug therapy management.

Time Management Skills

Success in almost any position requires the ability to set goals, prioritize tasks, and manage time. Interviewers will want to hear specific examples of how you manage your time and what tools you find useful, such as a daily calendar or personal data assistants. Make sure you can answer the following questions:

- Tell me about a time when you did not meet an important deadline. What steps have you taken to avoid this situation in the future?

- How much time did you devote to outside work while you were completing your pharmacy [college, high school] degree?

- What approach do you use for time management?

- Give me examples of how you prioritized work assignments in your most recent position. How do you keep them scheduled to meet deadlines?

- Tell me about a time you requested an extension to complete an important assignment.

- Tell me about a time when you completed an important assignment ahead of schedule.

- Describe your typical workday.

- How do you organize your daily assignments and activities?

- Give me an example of a time management skill that has increased your productivity at work.

- Tell me how you deal with procrastination.

Volunteerism

Your work as a volunteer provides evidence of your ability to share time and expertise with others. The skills you develop doing volunteer activities can also prove as valuable as those acquired through paid work. Prepare a list of your volunteer efforts, including professional organizations and community service projects, and think about how each experience has enhanced your career. In what ways might the things you learned as a volunteer contribute to the position you seek? Questions you may need to answer include:

- Tell me about your association with community service organizations. To what extent have you been involved?

- Have you held any positions in a community service organization? If so, to what extent were you involved? What did you gain from the experience?

- Have you ever been considered for a public office? What were the circumstances? What did you gain from the experience?

- Tell me about your involvement in extracurricular activities as a pharmacy student.

- What organizations did you belong to as a pharmacy student?

- Which organizations did you enjoy the most [least]?

- Our organization believes that employees should give time back to the community. How do you feel about this?

- What professional-based community projects interest you?

- Would you consider volunteering as a member of our organization if we did not hire you as an employee?

Concluding the Interview

Questions that interviewers use to wrap up the session can serve as effective segues into your own questions. Always have questions ready to ask if the opportunity comes up. Also, have at least one suitable response in mind if the interviewer asks "Is there anything else I should know about you?" or "Is there anything else I should ask?" Possible questions for concluding the interview include:

- In what respect do our position and your needs appear to be a good match? In what respect do they differ?

- Is there anything else I should ask?

- Is there anything that will keep you from taking this position if we offer it?

- When can you start work?

- Now that we have spent some time orienting you to the position, what level of interest do you have?

- How does this position compare with other positions you are considering?

DISCRIMINATORY QUESTIONS

Federal laws do not permit discriminatory questions about your race, color, religion, sex, national origin, marital status, age, or disability.* Although experienced interviewers do not usually ask illegal questions, inexperienced or improperly prepared interviewers might. You may choose to answer an illegal question if you think you can get by with an indirect response. For example, if asked about your plans for marriage you could say that you don't intend for your personal life to interfere with your work performance. Or, you could ask the interviewer to explain how this information relates to the position, and then give a similar response. Depending on the circumstances, a direct response such as "I would rather not answer that question" may suffice. Federal laws consider the following sample questions illegal:

- How old are you?
- What is your birth date?
- Are you a citizen of the United States?
- When did you become a citizen of the United States?
- Where were your parents born?
- What is your native language?
- What is your maiden name?
- Our staff is young. How do you think you will fit in?
- What is your religion?
- Does your religion keep you from working on weekends or holidays?
- Do you feel that your race will help you be more effective in this position?
- Who do you live with?
- What is your marital status?
- Where does your spouse work?
- What are your plans for starting a family?
- Other than traffic violations, have you ever committed an unlawful act?

- How many children do you have?
- You mentioned that you have two children. Would this keep you from overnight travel assignments?
- Can you make child care arrangements?
- What is your sexual preference?
- Have you ever been arrested?
- Would you prefer to be addressed as Miss or Mrs.?
- Did you receive an honorable discharge from the military service?
- How tall are you?
- How much do you weigh?
- Have you ever filed for bankruptcy?
- Do you have a good credit rating?
- Do you have any disabilities?
- What can you tell me about your medical history?
- Have you ever received workers' compensation?
- Have you ever been treated for alcoholism or drug dependence?
- Have you ever been hospitalized?
- Do you have any health conditions that would compromise your attendance record?
- How many days of work did you miss last year because of illness?
- Have you had any recent or past illnesses or operations?
- Do you belong to any social, religious, or community groups?

* *The relevant federal laws include: Title VII of the Civil Rights Act of 1964; Age Discrimination in Employment Act of 1967; Title I of the Americans with Disabilities Act of 1990; The Rehabilitation Act of 1973; The Vietnam Era Veteran's Readjustment Act of 1974; Executive Order 11246.*

QUESTIONING THE INTERVIEWER

Interviewers expect intelligent questions from successful candidates. The chance to ask questions generally occurs throughout the interview process, especially if the process is informal. Even in a formal interview process, an opportunity will arise when the interviewer invites questions. Make sure you ask questions relevant to the position. Before interviewing, prepare a written list of questions that you would like to have answered. You may choose to glance at the list during your interview session if you can't remember specific questions. You may also ask the interviewer if he or she minds if you take notes. The following list contains examples of questions you can ask:

- How often do you conduct performance evaluations?

- If I succeed in this position, what opportunities will I have to advance within the organization?

- What criteria will you use to evaluate my performance in this position?

- Does your organization support rewards and recognition for employees who exceed expectations?

- Do you feel that I have the qualifications needed for success in this position?

- How do you project the organization during the next one to three years?

- What relationship exists between this department and senior management?

- What attracted you to this organization?

- What do you like about working here?

- What organizational changes do you expect within the next year?

- How do the departments in the organization view this department?

- How receptive are other health professionals in your organization to clinical intervention recommendations by pharmacists?

- Do you encourage participation in community service and professional organizations?

- What do you consider the primary reason for your organization's success?

- Can I obtain a copy of the department's organizational chart to have a better understanding of where this position fits in?

- How does management respond to staff ideas?

- What immediate challenges face your department?

- What complaints get regularly voiced by your staff?

- What types of pharmacists [employees] generally succeed in your organization?

- What pharmacists will I work with? Can I meet them?

- I understand the last person in this position got promoted. Can I meet with him or her?

- How would you describe your management style?

- What personal qualities do you like most in your employees?

- What changes would you expect the next person who fills this position to make?

- Does your staff ever socialize outside work?

- Approximately what percentage of full-time positions filled in the past three years still exist in the organization?

- Was this position posted internally?

- To what extent do senior managers solicit ideas and invite feedback from staff members?

- Why is this position available?

- Is this a new position or will I be replacing someone?

- Can you describe a typical work day for someone in this position?

- What type of orientation will I receive if I am hired?

- Would I be responsible for supervising other staff? If so, how many and what positions?

- Where does this position fit into your organizational structure?

QUESTIONING THE INTERVIEWER *continued*

- What kinds of assignments should I anticipate during the first six months in the position?

- What aspect of this position do you consider most difficult?

- How many employees have held this position in the last three years?

- How many employees have been promoted from this position in the last three years?

- What did you like most about the person who previously held this position?

- What are your immediate priorities for the person who fills this position?

- Why is this position being filled with an external candidate?

- What are the three most critical elements of the position description for this position?

- What skills and abilities must a pharmacist taking this position demonstrate?

- How would you describe the ideal candidate for this position?

- Can I provide you with any additional information about me and my qualifications?

- When you think about employees who have succeeded in this position, what kind of qualities did they usually have?

- Are you concerned that I do not have an advanced degree?

- Do you have any concerns about my experience or skills?

- What opportunities exist for continuing my education?

- Have you experienced any staff reductions in the past three years?

- What is the turnover rate among pharmacists in your organization?

- Does your organization provide any financial assistance to attend professional meetings?

- Do you encourage employees to become active in professional associations?

- Have you faced any budget reductions during the past three years? If so, were there any reductions in staff?

- Do you expect any reductions in staff in the next year?

- What types of training and development do you provide for the advancement of an individual in this position?

- Do you have a tuition reimbursement program available? If so, how does it work?

- Do you have a management development program?

- What are the primary responsibilities associated with this position?

- What do pharmacists say about their overall satisfaction with your organization?

- What do your employees like most [least] about working here?

- What does a typical weekly schedule look like for this position?

- Who will be my supervisor if I am hired?

- What are the three most important criteria that you will use to select the candidate for this position?

- What are the most difficult adjustments new employees face when joining your department?

- What process do you use to determine the adequacy of resources for this position?

- How would you describe the department's culture?

- Will I have a standard benefits package or will I choose from a variety of options?

- Do you base salary adjustments on merit?

- What is the next step in the hiring process?

- Who will make the final hiring decision?

- How soon will you make a hiring decision?

- I am interested in this position. If I don't hear from you within the next week, may I call to see if you have made a decision?

Chapter 11

Types of Letters

When you send out a résumé or curriculum vitae, you also need to send a cover letter. Cover letters introduce you to your résumé recipient and help create an initial positive impression. As a marketing tool, the cover letter should highlight your qualifications, experience, and achievements and convince others that you deserve consideration.

The key question any employer ultimately wants answered is, "What can you do for us?" Cover letters are a great opportunity to highlight special skills and experience and suggest how they can be put to use in the position you're applying for.

When well written, your cover letter helps distinguish you from other potential candidates. Keep your cover letters concise, clear, and to the point. Think of them as a supplement to your résumé or CV that answers important questions in the reader's mind, such as:

- Why is this person writing?

- How well does his or her background meet the organization's needs?

- Does he or she have the qualifications needed for this position?

The Different Types of Job Search Letters

During your employment search process you may need to send out various types of letters. As a general rule of thumb, you should type your letters. Thank you notes are the one exception, since they seem more personal and genuine when they are handwritten. However, you can type thank you letters when a more formal style seems appropriate for the situation.

Position Availability Inquiries

To find out about an organization that interests you and to learn of available positions, consider sending a letter of inquiry. Begin by explaining the reason for your letter, and state that your research or familiarity with the organization's reputation has prompted you to write. Summarize the ways your major achievements could benefit the organization. Express your thanks and conclude the letter by noting your availability for an interview. Attach your résumé or CV to round out the package.

Responding to a Position Notice

To express your interest in a position that was announced in an ad or job notice, start by explaining your reason for writing and how you learned about the available position. Highlight your strengths and point out ways they meet the requirements listed for the position. You will probably want to review your résumé or CV to choose those qualities that most closely

---

ASPECTS OF GREAT COVER LETTERS

To make your cover letter most effective:

- Address it to someone who has the authority to hire you. Use the person's name and title, spelled correctly.

- Remain as brief and focused as possible.

- Tell how you became attracted to the company or opportunity. Show that you've done some homework on the company by indicating that you understand their current problems, interests, or priorities.

- Convey your enthusiasm for the opportunity you seek.

- Balance a professional tone with touches of personal warmth. You don't want to sound like a machine.

- Outline specifically what you're looking for and what you can offer.

match the stated requirements, but don't repeat wording verbatim. Instead, include your résumé or CV in the package. Before closing the letter, note your availability for an interview.

Requesting a Reference

Sometimes you will need a letter of recommendation from your references—people who can vouch for your skills and background and have agreed to be contacted. Although some potential employers prefer to make direct contact with references themselves, others will ask you to supply written letters. Obtain these letters as soon as possible. Write a cover letter that expresses your appreciation for the person's willingness to serve as reference and include the following information:

- Your résumé or CV.

- A copy of the position announcement or description of duties.

- A statement highlighting your additional qualifications relevant to the position.

- Specific contact information.

- A deadline for completing the reference.

Sometimes references will need to send their letters of recommendation directly to the employer. Other times you may need to submit the letters along with an application. In the second circumstance, ask each person preparing a reference to seal the letter in an envelope and sign his or her name across the sealed flap. Provide the reference with an addressed, stamped envelope for returning the recommendation to you or the employer.

SEVEN WAYS TO RUIN YOUR COVER LETTER

1. Spell the company's name incorrectly.

2. Send the letter to the wrong address.

3. Address the letter "Dear Sir" even when the hiring authority is a woman.

4. Misspell words and make typographical errors.

5. Use poor grammar.

6. Forget to enclose your résumé.

7. Omit your telephone number.

Confirming an Interview

Sending a potential employer a letter confirming your interview appointment furthers the positive impression you've already made through your résumé, letters, and phone calls. It also demonstrates your attention to detail. Keep the letter very brief. Begin by expressing your appreciation for the opportunity to interview. Then simply confirm the date, time, and location.

> **TIP:** Letters are more effective when addressed to a specific person. If necessary, call the organization to get the appropriate contact name and the correct spelling.

Thanking the Interviewer

After an interview, send a follow-up letter expressing your thanks, preferably within three days. Your letter should indicate your continuing interest in the position and highlight any specific areas that you consider relevant, based on discussions during the interview process. You may choose to comment briefly about individuals you met, available resources, or other aspects of the interview that left you with a favorable impression. As you draw the letter to a close, mention your understanding of the next step in the hiring process and indicate your willingness to provide any additional information.

Even if you do not want to pursue the position, you should still send a polite letter of thanks. Thank the person for the opportunity to interview for the position and request that they withdraw your application from further consideration.

Declining an Interview

Sometimes you might send in an application for a position or initiate a request for an interview (perhaps by sending a letter of inquiry) and before specific interview plans get set, your priorities change. If you find you no longer want to pursue the position, send the interviewer a polite letter requesting that they withdraw your application. This displays your professionalism. Even if you have already indicated over the phone that you no longer want the position, a letter makes it official and eliminates potential confusion between you and the interviewer.

Postponing a Decision

If you need extra time to make up your mind about accepting a position, discuss it over the phone with the employer and follow up with a letter. Begin by expressing your *continued* interest in the position and your appreciation for receiving an offer. Then state your need to postpone a decision. You can decide whether or not to include the specific reason you need additional time. Some possible reasons include evaluating other offers, assessing the compensation package, or discussing the pros and cons of relocating with your family. In the letter, let the recipient know the date when you will provide a decision. In the conclusion, note your appreciation for the employers' cooperation and understanding.

Declining a Position Offer

If you can't accept a position, send a letter declining the offer as soon as you reach your final decision. If appropriate, you can state your reason for declining the offer, but this isn't necessary. Include a polite closing statement expressing your appreciation for the organization's consideration.

Accepting a Position Offer

When writing an acceptance letter, sound gracious, professional, and enthusiastic. State that you accept the offer and appreciate the opportunity to become part of the company or organization. Confirm your official start date and any other relevant details. Conclude with an expression of thanks.

Chapter 12

Preparing Letters

When you write cover letters and other correspondence related to pharmacy opportunities, always adhere to standard business letter style. You can find good books in your local library or bookstore that describe the business letter format.

The most commonly used business letter styles include the block, modified block, and modified semi-block. Figures 10.1, 10.2, and 10.3 show examples of these styles.[1] Health professionals routinely use the block style.

Try to write in a positive tone and use the active voice as much a possible (see sidebar on page 130). Pay attention to the details in your letter and proofread it carefully for spelling, typing, punctuation, and grammatical errors.

Elements of a Standard Letter

Letterhead

Before preparing your letters, create a standard letterhead with your name and address. You can also include your telephone number and e-mail address. Usually, the letterhead gets centered at the top of the page. For electronic communications, however, you may want to place the letterhead flush with the left margin to avoid a formatting conflict.

Margins

In all business letters, set the left, right, top, and bottom margins at one inch or greater.

> **TIP:** Before you seal the envelope and mail your letter, proofread the contents again. Remember that your cover letter must create a positive impression to help advance you to the next level of evaluation.

Dateline

Type the dateline approximately three lines below the last line of the letterhead, although you can allow more space depending on the letter's length.

On the dateline, note the month, day, and year (e.g., July 24, 2006). Make sure to place a comma between the day and year. Another variation, especially in government-related communications, begins with the day in numeral form, followed by the month and year (e.g., 24 July 2006).

In block letters, place the dateline flush with the left margin. In modified block or modified semi-block letters, place it right of the page's center.

Recipient Address

You can precede the recipient's name with a courtesy title (e.g., Dr., Mr., Ms.), unless you follow the name by an abbreviation of his or her degree. Do not put both a courtesy title and a degree. List the recipient's title and name as it appears on correspondence you have received from the person. Make sure you spell everything correctly.

If you cannot identify the contact's name, list the name of the department or unit within the organization, followed by the standard mailing address, city, state, and zip code. Verify the accuracy of a five- or nine-digit zip code by checking the United States Postal Service's Web site at www.framed.usps.com.

Salutation

Type the letter's salutation two lines below the last line of the recipient's address and flush with the left margin. Follow it with a colon.

Avoid using the impersonal introductions of "Dear Sir or Madam" or "Dear Director of Pharmacy." Reserve these generic salutations for times when you have exhausted all reasonable approaches for finding the name of the specific contact person. It's usually easy to call the organization and ask the secretary for the contact's name, title, and correct spelling.

Body

The body of the letter follows two lines below the salutation. Single space each line within a paragraph. Between paragraphs, use a double space. In block and modified block letters, keep all lines of each paragraph flush with the left margin. For modified semi-block letters, indent the initial line of each paragraph 5 to 10 spaces.

As explained in Chapter 11, Types of Letters, the first paragraph of the letter indicates your interest in the position and states how you learned about it. The second paragraph highlights your qualifications and experience and notes how they match the position requirements. In this paragraph, you should also refer the reader to your résumé or curriculum vitae for additional detail. The final paragraph mentions your willingness to arrange an interview and thanks the contact person for considering you for the position.

If your letter exceeds one page, begin the second page with a heading (flush with the left margin) that includes the name of the person receiving the letter, the date, and the page number.

USE THE ACTIVE VOICE

The active voice is more direct, emphatic, and vigorous than the passive voice. In the active voice, the subject of the sentence does the action: "George Washington chopped down the cherry tree." In the passive voice, the subject receives the action: "The cherry tree was chopped down by George Washington."

Besides being boring, the passive voice can leave out important details. For example, if you say, "Savings were gained from improvements in operations," the reader has no idea who made the improvements or brought about the savings. You can use the passive voice occasionally—if, for example, it doesn't matter who performed the action—but use it sparingly.

Complimentary Close

Place the complimentary close two lines after the end of the body. In a block letter, the complimentary close appears flush with the left margin. In a modified block or semi-block letter, align the close under the dateline. Capitalize the first letter of the complimentary close only, and insert a comma at the end. Typical examples for business correspondence include: Respectfully, Respectfully yours, Very truly yours, Best regards, Most sincerely, Sincerely, and Sincerely yours. You can choose the complimentary close you like best.

> **TIP:** For best results, print your letter on quality paper using a laser printer. Never use wrinkled or torn paper. You can use an ink jet printer if it produces high-quality results, but stay away from dot matrix printers.

Signature Block

Type the signature block approximately four lines beneath and in direct line with the complimentary close. Spell out your name as it appears in your formal signature and letterhead.

Enclosures

Place a notation that acknowledges any enclosures flush with the left margin. You can use the word "Enclosure" or an abbreviation such as "Encl." If you have several enclosures, put the specific number before the "Enclosure" notation, or note it afterwards in parentheses. You can follow the notation with a colon and a brief description of the enclosure.

The Envelope

Envelope Size

Although most people routinely use an envelope with the dimensions of 4 1/8 x 9 1/2 inches (a #10 commercial envelope) for mailing letters, consider using an envelope that measures 9 x 12 inches. Larger and roomier, this size envelope is less likely to put noticeable creases in your cover letter and résumé or CV, and it may stand out in the recipient's stack of mail.

Figure 10.1 Block letter 131

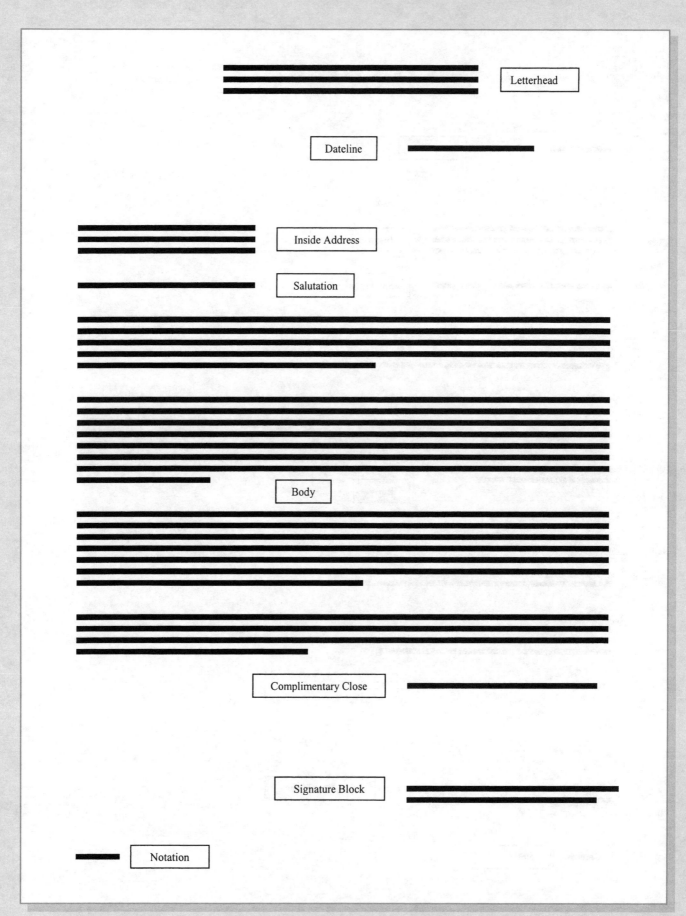

Figure 10.3 Modified semi-block letter 133

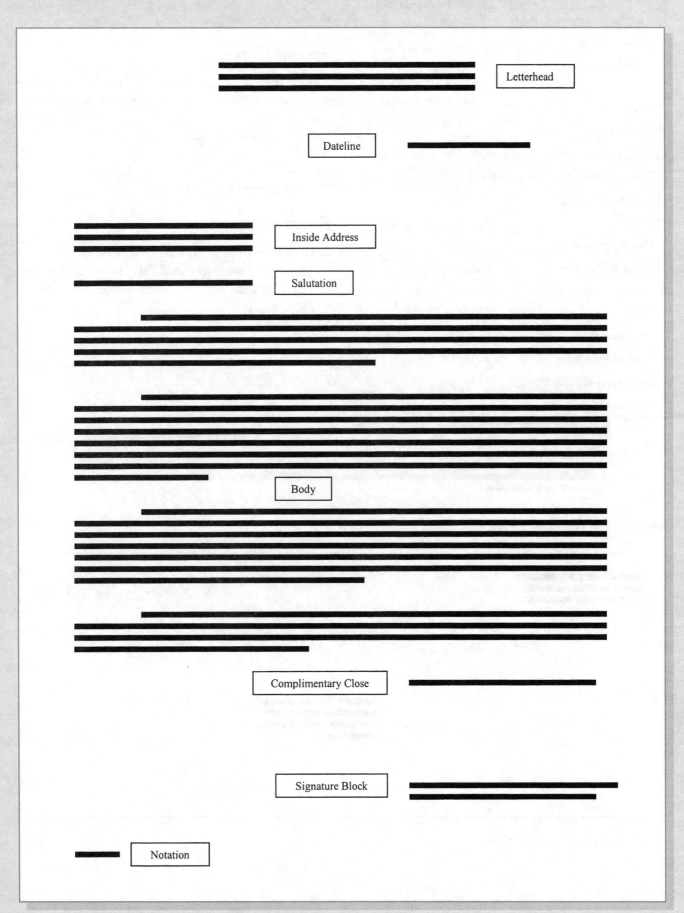

Actual letter size is 8.5 x 11

> **TIP:** If you want to include a special mailing notation (e.g., certified mail, registered mail, personal, confidential) on your letter, capitalize it and place it approximately four lines below the dateline, flush with the left margin. Put the same notation on the envelope roughly four spaces above the first line of the addressee's name.

Return Address

Place your name and return address—identical to the information that appears in your letterhead—in the upper left quadrant of the envelope. Figure 10.4 shows a standard business envelope and address placement.

Recipient Address

When addressing an envelope, always use the same address information contained in the letter. The addressee's name and address should begin at the approximate center of the envelope. Common word processing software will prepare a postal-approved bar code for the Zip Code (5 digit or Zip+4).

If desired, you can select this function when preparing the addressee's mailing address.

Special Notations

Place special mailing notations approximately four spaces above the first line of the addressee's name. Type these notations in all capital letters. The special notations "personal" and "confidential" usually get placed to the upper left of the addressee's name, while "certified," "registered," or "special delivery" are placed to the upper right.

Reference

1. Lindsell-Roberts S, Stevens MA. In: *Merriam Webster's Secretarial Handbook*. 3rd ed. Springfield, Massachusetts: Merriam-Webster, Inc; 1993:244-289.

Figure 10.4 Business Envelope

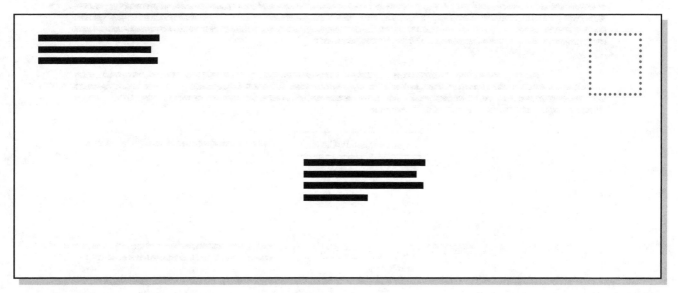

Actual envelope size is 4.125 x 9.5

Chapter 13

Sample Letters

This chapter provides sample letters to give you an idea of effective formats and wording. The letters serve various purposes, including responding to job announcements, seeking applications, confirming interviews, inquiring about internships, and expressing thanks. Just like the sample résumés and CVs in this book, the letters provide examples only. You must tailor your own letters to your individual needs and circumstances.

When you draft a letter, use the guidelines that follow to help you prepare final copy that meets professional standards.

Guidelines for Letter Format

- Adhere to customary business letter style and format.

- Use a standard letterhead with your name and address.

- Include your telephone number as part of your standard letterhead. Otherwise, make sure to include it in the body of the letter.

- Place your letterhead symmetrically at the top of the page.

- Follow a consistent letter style (i.e., block, modified block, or modified semi-block).

- Set all margins at one inch or greater.

- For block letters, type the dateline approximately three lines below the last line of the letterhead and flush with the left margin. For modified block or modified semi-block letters, put the dateline right of center or flush with the right margin.

- Place special mailing notations such as certified mail, registered mail, personal, or confidential in capital letters approximately four lines below the dateline, flush with the left margin.

- In the inside address, include the name and address of the receiver followed by the standard mailing address, city, state, and zip code.

- Type the letter's salutation two lines beneath the last line of the inside address and flush with the left margin.

- Follow the salutation by a colon.

- In the body of the letter, use single spaced paragraphs, with a double space between each paragraph.

- In block and modified block letters, keep the lines of each paragraph flush left. In modified semi-block letters, indent the initial line of each paragraph 5 to 10 spaces.

- Use the active voice and a positive tone throughout your letter.

COVER LETTERS WITH RÉSUMÉS

The cover letter you send with your résumé or CV allows you to highlight special skills, share relevant personal information, and emphasize the benefits you can bring to the employer or organization. Always present yourself in a positive light and follow these rules:

- State the position you are applying for.

- Summarize your qualifications.

- Describe how you can meet the organization's needs and what you can accomplish for the organization. Employers are far more interested in what you can do for them than in the benefits you seek.

- Show some knowledge of the company or institution by weaving in accurate details.

- Sound polite, yet confident.

- Mention that your résumé is enclosed and indicate your desire to meet with the employer.

- Review the content of your letter for spelling, typing, punctuation, and grammatical errors.

- If the content of your letter exceeds one page, begin the second page with a heading that includes the name of the person receiving the letter, the date, and the page number.

- Place the complimentary close two lines after the last line of the letter's body. In a block letter, keep it flush with the left margin. In a modified or semi-modified block letter, align the complimentary close under the dateline.

- Capitalize only the first letter of the complimentary close, and place a comma at the end.

- Type the signature block approximately four lines beneath, and aligned with, the complimentary close.

- If you use a notation (e.g., "Enclosure" or "Encl.") to acknowledge additional items in the envelope, type it flush with the left margin. You may follow the notation with a colon and a brief description of the enclosure.

- Print the final letter using quality paper and a laser printer. Try to use paper with the same quality as your résumé or CV.

Tips on Writing Letters

Chapters 11 and 12 highlight types of letters and standard formats to put you well on your way toward preparing professional correspondence. But what about the writing itself? When composing a letter, your goal is always to communicate clearly. Good writing is simple, which means it reads well, is easy to follow, and does not contain unnecessary words. Even complex ideas can be expressed with short words and succinct paragraphs.

Many people in business and academia are used to reading documents choked with clutter. The sentences are overly complicated and full of extra-long words and redundant phrases. It's hard to figure out what the writer is trying to say. But seeing how common such writing is, people think they must imitate this inflated style to sound intelligent and fit in to their chosen community. Here are a few communication techniques to remember:

- Be brief and to the point.

- State your purpose in the first paragraph. This will focus your reader and keep his or her attention.

Table 13.1 Ways to Simplify Wordy Phrases

Wordy Phrase	Condensed Phrase
in the event that	if
in light of the fact that	since
be considered that	is
start off	start
exhibits the ability to	can
on an annual basis	yearly
for the purpose of	for
on the occasion of	when
in the final analysis	finally
it is obvious that	obviously
on an everyday basis	routinely
despite the fact that	although
in the proximity of	near
subsequent to	later

- Use a natural tone in your writing. Don't try to sound like someone you're not. Of course you must use good grammar and the right level of formality for your audience—no slang or off-color words—but avoid sounding fake or pretentious.

- Never use long words when short words work well. For example, instead of "facilitate" say "help" or "ease." Instead of "numerous" say "many."

- Prune excess words. Unnecessary words slow the reader and smother your message. A sentence is wordy if it can be tightened without loss of meaning. Table 13-1 gives examples of wordy phrases and ways you can condense them.

- Do not smother verbs. Sometimes excellent verbs are smothered in sentences because they are presented as nouns. For example, instead of saying "make a decision" it is more effective to say "decide." Instead of "establish a connection" say "connect."

- Use clichés sparingly or not at all. Clichés are trite, overused expressions, such as "light as a feather" or "hit the nail on the head." Whenever you are tempted to use a cliché, ask yourself if there is a more effective way to make your point.

- Review, revise, and polish after you write your first draft. No one crafts a perfect letter the first time through. If the stakes are high—such as when you are applying for a position you really want—don't ruin your chances with sloppy, unclear writing.

This cover letter in response to a job announcement for a pharmacy technician is positive, clear, and direct. Font: Times New Roman 12 point.

Lauren G. Smith ━━━━━━━━━━━━━━━━━━━━
4501 Canyon Boulevard • Ogden, Utah 84403 • (801) 621-9469

October 15, 2005

Pamela Davis, R.Ph.
Davidson's Pharmacy
210 W. 200 South
Salt Lake City, Utah 84120

Note how she emphasizes her strengths.

Dear Ms. Davis:

This letter is in response to your announcement of a pharmacy technician position opening in the October 14th edition of the *Salt Lake Tribune*. A copy of my résumé is enclosed.

I am looking for a position that will allow me to use my people skills and attention to detail in a community pharmacy setting in the Salt Lake City area. Although most of my experience is in the inpatient setting at Great Canyon Hospital, I have eight months of recent experience in the hospital's ambulatory care clinic pharmacy. In that position I received accolades for my ability to interact in a positive, helpful way with elderly patients and people feeling stressed by their pain or illness.

I am impressed by the varied programs you offer, including your asthma clinic, cholesterol screenings, and compounding services. I would find it rewarding to serve on the staff of a progressive pharmacy such as yours.

I will contact you during the next week to arrange a convenient time to meet. Thank you in advance for considering my request.

Sincerely,

Lauren G. Smith

Enclosure

It's good that she shows initiative here; she should be sure to follow through and make contact, as promised.

A short, readable request for an application to a Doctor of Pharmacy program. Font: Arial 12 point.

Danielle Shaffer
1201 Ryan Street
New Castle, Pennsylvania 16105
(717) 258-4473
deshaffer@netlink.com

August 22, 2005

Would be better to include a contact name, especially since the writer is serious enough about this school to request a meeting.

Office of Admissions
School of Pharmacy
University of Pittsburgh
1104 Salk Hall
Pittsburgh, Pennsylvania 15266

Dear Director of Admissions:

I am currently a student at Gettysburg College, where I am completing prerequisite courses for a Doctor of Pharmacy degree.

Please send me an application for admission to your program beginning in autumn 2006. Additionally, I would like to meet with you to review my academic plan and arrange a tour of your campus.

I will call soon to set up an appointment. If you would like to reach me in the meantime, my contact information is above. Thank you for accommodating my request.

Sincerely,

Danielle Shaffer

This request for an application to a nontraditional Doctor of Pharmacy program is businesslike and to the point. Font: Georgia 12 point.

Monica N. Sims, R.Ph.
7453 Sunset Circle
St. Louis, Missouri 63123

It's helpful to include full contact information, including telephone number and e-mail address.

March 10, 2005

Director of Admissions
School of Pharmacy and Allied Health Professions
Creighton University
2200 Nebraska Plaza
Omaha, Nebraska 68348-0545

Would be more effective to address this to a specific person.

Dear Director:

After five years of pharmacy practice, I am interested in changing my career path. Would you please send me an application for admission to your nontraditional Doctor of Pharmacy program?

I look forward to your response.

Sincerely,

Monica N. Sims

This inquiry about internship openings provides clear details and good information to "sell" the candidate.
Font: Georgia 12 point.

Lorraine M. Meyer

7225 Pine Tree Place
Omaha, Nebraska 68116

Telephone: 402.431.9664
E-mail: lmm387@neb.edu

January 15, 2006

Ms. Kimberly Ferguson
Albertsons Inc.
General Offices
460 Sumpterfield Drive
Boise, Idaho 83682

Dear Ms. Ferguson:

This paragraph lets the reader know that the writer has done background research on the company. It highlights strengths of the candidate that may not appear on the résumé and links them to company values.

I am completing the second year of a Doctor of Pharmacy degree program at the University of Nebraska College of Pharmacy. My goal for the summer of 2006 is to obtain a pharmacy internship in a community pharmacy that offers disease management and other patient-oriented services.

Dr. Lindsey Elliott, my faculty mentor, told me that you may have internship openings in the Lincoln area. I will return to Lincoln at the end of the academic year and will be available for employment from June 1 through August 15, 2006. I am registered as a pharmacy intern with the Nebraska Board of Pharmacy. A copy of my résumé is enclosed for your review.

My values are very much in line with those of Albertsons, including emphasizing community citizenship and always striving to improve. For two years on Saturday mornings I have tutored three teenage Sudanese refugees in English, math, and science. I am known for seeking feedback from professors and peers to help me improve my skills, and people often compliment me on my positive attitude.

I would appreciate being considered for an internship position and will call you next week to follow up about next steps in the application process. Thank you for your attention.

Sincerely,

Lorraine M. Meyer

After highlighting her interest in the internship and her background, she politely alerts the recipient that she will be calling next week.

Actual letter size is 8.5 x 11

In requesting an interview at a Residency Showcase, this writer is succinct and courteous, but the letter could be better organized. Font: Times New Roman 12 point.

Grant D. Hayes

1320 Sunset Place	Residence: (785) 865-9037
Lawrence, KS 66094	Cellular: (785) 334-8072
grant.hayes@zipnet.com	Fax: (785) 865-9054

November 3, 2005

A busy reader might not continue further to realize that the writer is seeking more than written information. He could move the second sentence to the next paragraph.

Michael A. Strickland, Pharm.D.
Pharmacy Residency Program Director
Department of Pharmacy
Thomas Jefferson University Hospital
141 South 10th Street
Philadelphia, PA 19107-5098

Dear Dr. Strickland:

I am completing the final year of a doctor of pharmacy degree program at the University of Kansas School of Pharmacy. I have ten years of experience as a pharmacy technician in the United States Navy and more recently as a pharmacy intern at the University of Kansas Medical Center. Could you please send information about your residency program to my address above?

I am seeking a pharmacy practice residency to help achieve my career goal of practicing in a health-system pharmacy. Next month, when I attend the ASHP Midyear Clinical Meeting in Las Vegas, I hope to speak with you about your program at the Residency Showcase. Receiving information in advance will help me prepare for a productive discussion.

My résumé is enclosed to apprise you of my skills and experience. I look forward to meeting you in Las Vegas.

Sincerely,

Grant D. Hayes

Enclosure

To ensure a meeting, the writer should consider asking for a specific appointment and should say he will call to set one up, which shows initiative.

It would be better for the writer to state in the first paragraph that he is seeking a meeting at the showcase so the recipient understands immediately.

Actual letter size is 8.5 x 11

A request for an application to a residency program. Font: CG Omega 12 point.

Erin B. Rogers
8559 Hunter Drive
Memphis, TN 38118
901.547.8995
ebrogers@silvernet.com

October 18, 2005

> In the first paragraph, it's helpful to state the reason for writing. She could move her interests and qualifications to the second paragraph.

Rodney J. Harrison, Pharm.D.
University of California at San Francisco
521 Parnasus Avenue, Room A 194
San Francisco, CA 94143-0608

Dear Dr. Harrison:

I am completing a pharmacy practice residency program at the Regional Medical Center in Memphis. During my residency and Doctor of Pharmacy program, I have gained experience in working with oncology patients. I enjoy the challenges of this patient population and plan to pursue a specialized residency in oncology pharmacy practice.

I have enclosed my curriculum vitae for your review and would appreciate receiving an application for your residency program. I will attend the upcoming meetings of the American College of Clinical Pharmacy and the American Society of Health-System Pharmacists and hope to meet with you to discuss the possibility of pursuing your specialized residency. Through your residency program I seek to enhance my skills in providing pharmaceutical care, conducting clinical research, spearheading patient education programs, and developing inservice training for staff.

During the next week I will contact your office to see if I can arrange a brief session with you at either the ACCP or ASHP meeting. Thank you in advance for considering my request.

Sincerely,

> It's good that she spells out specifics she hopes to learn in the residency, which suggests she knows something about the program. She should state in one more sentence why this particular residency is especially attractive to her.

Erin B. Rogers

Enclosure

Actual letter size is 8.5 x 11

A cover letter inquiring about a drug information fellowship that does a good job of getting right to the point. Font: Century Gothic 12 point.

DAVID K. REED

4416 Hawthorne Place   (215) 879-5135
Philadelphia, PA 19131   dkreed32@usip.edu

November 14, 2005

Brenda A. Miller, Pharm.D.
Associate Professor of Pharmacy
Rutgers, the State University of New Jersey
College of Pharmacy
242 Frelinguysen Road
Piscataway, NJ 08855-0634

The font chosen is a bit hard to read.

Dear Dr. Miller:

My advisor, Dr. Julia Narducci, recommended that I contact you about the drug information fellowship offered jointly by your college and Bristol-Myers Squibb. I will graduate in May 2006 with a Doctor of Pharmacy degree from the Philadelphia College of Pharmacy at the University of the Sciences in Philadelphia and would welcome the opportunity to meet with you at your convenience to discuss your fellowship.

During the past three years I have gained experience in the area of drug information services through my internships and clerkships, as outlined on the enclosed curriculum vitae. One of my clerkships focused on drug informatics, an area I particularly enjoy because of my aptitude for information management technology. I am also sending you three writing samples of drug information monographs I prepared for the Presbyterian Hospital's Department of Pharmacy Services.

I will call next week to arrange an appointment. Thank you for your time.

Sincerely,

David K. Reed

Enclosures

Nice the way that he highlights an area of particular interest.

A cover letter in response to an ad for a hospital pharmacist. Font: Times New Roman 12 point.

ALEXIS SEAY

8602 Kenyon Boulevard
Seattle, WA 98136
(206) 923-6813
amseay@landnet.com

June 2, 2005

Ms. Judith Jennings
Department of Human Resources
Denali Center/Fairbanks Hospital
3570 Landover Street
Fairbanks, Alaska 99605

Dear Ms. Jennings:

The typo here is a problem, suggesting to the reader that the writer does not pay attention to detail. Careful proofreading is essential.

I am responding to your recent advertisement in *Pharmacy Today* for a staff pharmacist with infusion therapy experience. I am a recent graduate of the University of Washington School of Pharmacy with part-time employment experience at Home Infusion Services, Inc. in Seattle. A copy of my curriculum vitae is attached.

As a native of Alaska, I am interested in relocating to the Fairbanks area. I would appreciate arranging an appointment to discuss the details of this position. I will be in the Seattle area until June 15th and can be contacted at the above address. I plan to return to return to Alaska by June 22nd. After this date, my address will be: 110 Caribou Circle, Big Delta, Alaska 99736. I will be able to be reached by telephone at (907) 457-3188 and my e-mail address will remain unchanged.

If possible, I would like to arrange an interview when your schedule permits. Thank you in advance for considering my request.

Sincerely,

Although her request for an interview is courteous, the approach is passive, leaving it up to the interviewer to take the initiative.

Alexis Seay, Pharm.D.

Enclosure

Actual letter size is 8.5 x 11

A concise, effective cover letter following up on a phone inquiry about a position. Font: Arial 12 point.

Allison Kay Wells, Pharm.D., M.B.A.

4726 Preston Drive
Dallas, TX 75240
(972) 239-1875
akwells@aol.com

April 2, 2005

Great that she writes the same day as the conversation, reinforcing her interest.

Suzanne Harrison, Regional Director
Blue Cross Blue Shield of Massachusetts
300 Newton Street
Boston, MA 02114

Dear Ms. Harrison:

As we discussed this morning, my family and I plan to move to the Boston area within the next two months. I have four years of experience developing and managing clinical programs associated with pharmacy benefit management plans. I would like to explore the opportunities of a similar position at Blue Cross Blue Shield of Massachusetts.

I am enclosing a copy of my curriculum vitae for your review. I understand that you may have an opening in the near future and would appreciate being considered for the position. I will call you in the next two weeks to set up an interview time that is convenient for you.

Sincerely,

Allison Kay Wells, Pharm.D., M.B.A.

Enclosure: Curriculum vitae

A gracious request for a letter of reference. Font: Verdana 12 point.

Austin D. Walker ━━━━━━━━━━━━━━━━━━

5028 Highland Park Drive   414-352-4225
Milwaukee, WI 53217   adwalker@aol.com

January 12, 2005

James R. Rutherford, Ph.D.
Professor, Pharmaceutical Sciences
School of Pharmacy
University of Wisconsin
425 N. Charter Street
Madison, WI 53706-1584

It's helpful that he provides a stamped envelope and lets the recipient know the deadline.

Dear Dr. Rutherford:

I enjoyed our brief telephone conversation this afternoon and I appreciate your words of encouragement concerning my interest in pursuing graduate studies. Thank you for your willingness to serve as a reference.

I have enclosed a copy of my curriculum vitae and the reference form requested by the Office of Graduate Admissions at the University of Texas. Also, I have included an addressed and stamped envelope for your convenience. The deadline for submitting my completed application to the University of Texas is March 1, 2005.

I will keep you informed about the status of my admission. Again, I appreciate the time and effort to complete a reference on my behalf.

Best regards,

Austin D. Walker

Actual letter size is 8.5 x 11

Cover letter in response to an announcement about an assistant professor position. Font: Georgia 12 point.

Janette L. Walker, Pharm.D.

8716 Fuller Drive   (518) 432-7384
Albany, New York 12206   jlwalker@empirenet.com

July 9, 2005

> *She should note how her experience will benefit the school if she is hired. What is special about her qualifications and experience, and how do they match the needs of the position?*

John H. Turner, Pharm.D.
Professor and Chair
Department of Pharmacy Practice
State University of New York at Buffalo
Amherst, New York 14180

Dear Dr. Turner:

I have enclosed a copy of my curriculum vitae in response to a recent announcement in the *AACP Report* for an assistant professor position at your School of Pharmacy.

I believe my faculty experience in ambulatory care could benefit your academic programs. My qualifications and experience are consistent with the position description in the announcement. Additionally, the opportunity to pursue a tenure track position is appealing.

I would welcome an invitation to meet with you to discuss the position in greater detail. I may be reached at the above address.

Thank you for your consideration.

Sincerely,

> *Her closing is passive and does not demonstrate initiative.*

> *It's nice that tenure track appeals to her, but this fact isn't going to sell the employer on her as a candidate. More important to use this space emphasizing her strengths.*

Janette L. Walker, Pharm.D.

Enclosure: Curriculum vitae

A courteous, readable acceptance letter for a position. Font: Verdana 12 point.

Courtney K. Moore, Pharm.D.

3664 Salem Boulevard ▪ Elizabeth, New Jersey 07206 ▪ 908.965.3108

A professional, concise, readable letter.

June 12, 2005

Brian J. Sheridan, Pharm.D.
Director of Operations
HLM Managed Care, Inc.
1835 Carlton Pike
Cherry Hill, New Jersey 08036

Dear Dr. Sheridan:

This letter serves as my formal acceptance of your offer to join HLM Managed Care, Inc. as a clinical account manager. I accept the conditions of employment outlined in your letter of June 4, 2005.

As requested, I will contact the Human Resources Division to complete all required application information.

I have tendered my resignation with my current employer, effective July 15, 2005. I will be able to meet the August 1, 2005 start date specified in your letter.

Again, thank you for providing me with this unique opportunity. I look forward to working with you and the other members of your department.

Best regards,

Courtney K. Moore, Pharm.D.

A request to be withdrawn from consideration for a position. Font: Century Schoolbook 12 point.

Louisa C. Morales, Pharm.D.

513 Lynnhurst Terrace
Los Angeles, California 90043

Telephone: (323) 293-2342
E-mail:lcmorales@cedarnet.com

March 12, 2005

A polite letter that leaves a good impression, which is a plus should they cross paths again.

Lauren Patterson, Pharm.D.
Clinical Coordinator
Department of Pharmacy
University of California
Irvine Medical Center
218 South Medical Drive
Orange, California 92558

Dear Dr. Patterson:

Thank you for the opportunity to meet with you to discuss your clinical pharmacist position. I appreciate the courtesy you and your staff extended during my informative visit.

As we discussed during the interview, I am attempting to balance my personal and professional goals in seeking a position. Based on my inability to accommodate a rotating schedule, I ask that you withdraw my candidacy from further consideration.

I was impressed with your organization and know that I would enjoy being a member of your staff. You have my best wishes for a successful search.

Sincerely,

Louisa C. Morales, Pharm.D.

A request for withdrawal of an application. Font: CG Times 12 point.

Jonathan H. Elliott, Pharm.D.
4840 Naylor Drive
Washington, D.C. 20009
(202) 483-9664
jonathan.elliott@horizon.com

March 15, 2005

Tricia E. Hall, Director
Department of Pharmacy
St. Elizabeth Medical Center
4300 East Avenue
Bridgeport, Connecticut 06604

Even when you're not interested in a position after applying, it's important to convey a positive attitude, as this writer does.

Dear Ms. Hall:

Thank you for the opportunity to meet with you and your staff to discuss my qualifications in filling a clinical coordinator position. I appreciate the courtesy and hospitality you extended during my stay in Bridgeport.

After thoughtful consideration, I ask that you withdraw my application from further consideration. My decision is primarily based on the inability of my spouse to relocate at this time.

Again, thank you for the time you spent informing me about your impressive organization.

Sincerely,

Jonathan H. Elliott, Pharm.D.

Actual letter size is 8.5 x 11

A letter confirming the time and date for an interview and noting that a CV is enclosed. Font: Arial 12 point.

Tyler R. Owens, R.Ph.

2410 Willow Drive • Chesapeake, VA 23322   • 757.482.5993 • trowens@erols.com

---

September 26, 2005

> *This letter says exactly what it needs to, and no more.*

Francis L. Wood, Pharm.D.
Director of Pharmacy Services
Albright Medical Center
Victoria, Virginia 23184

Dear Dr. Wood:

Thank you for giving me an opportunity to interview with you and your staff on Monday, October 3rd at 9:00 a.m. in your office. As requested, I have attached a copy of my curriculum vitae. Please let me know if you need additional information about my qualifications and experience. I appreciate your consideration and look forward to meeting you.

Sincerely,

Tyler R. Owens, R.Ph.

Encl.

A thank you letter following an interview. Font: Lucida Bright 12 point.

Matthew D. Briggs, M.S., R.Ph.

7045 Cooper Drive
Columbus, GA 31907
(706) 563-4226
mdbriggs@aol.com

April 16, 2004

Matthew K. Blake, Pharm.D.
Cardinal Health Nuclear Pharmacy Services
3712 Barrow Street
Nashville, TN 37205

Nice the way he emphasizes his interest in the position.

Dear Dr. Blake:

Thank you for the opportunity to interview with you and your staff. I appreciate the time and effort you spent in organizing this informative session.

I am very interested in joining your nuclear pharmacy staff and contributing my skills to your high-quality operation. I am impressed by your emphasis on efficiency and innovative services. Please let me know if you need additional information about my qualifications or experience. I look forward to hearing from you.

Sincerely,

Matthew D. Briggs, M.S., R.Ph.

A letter declining an interview for a residency. Font: Times New Roman 14.

Tracey N. Jennings
1424 Lewis Street
Boston, Massachusetts 02114

In declining an interview, this writer's tone is gracious, and she gives a clear reason without belaboring it.

February 4, 2005

Lia Chang, Pharm.D.
Pharmacy Residency Program Director
Veterans Affairs Medical Center
84 Oak Street
Rochester, New York 14738

Dear Dr. Chang:

Thank you for extending an invitation to interview for your pharmacy practice residency. After reassessing my career goals, I have decided to seek employment rather than a residency position in the coming year. You have my best wishes for a successful search.

Sincerely,

Tracey N. Jennings

A thank you letter following an interview. Font: Garamond 14 point.

Laura K. Ross, R.Ph.

9640 Pine Street
Providence, Rhode Island 02907
(401) 785-8968
lkross@zipnet.com

August 14, 2005

Shelly Peterson, R.Ph.
Recruitment Director
CVS Corporation
1 CVS Drive
Woonsocket, Rhode Island 02836

Dear Ms. Peterson:

Thank you for the opportunity to interview with you and your colleagues yesterday. The goals of your organization closely match my career interests. I left with a positive impression.

The writer misses an opportunity here to reiterate her career interests and emphasize how her strengths will benefit the organization.

I am very interested in pursing the position and working with your organization. I look forward to hearing from you soon.

Sincerely,

Laura K. Ross, R.Ph.

Thank you letter to a person who served as a reference. Font: Verdana 12 point.

Courtney K. Moore, Pharm.D.

3664 Salem Boulevard ▪ Elizabeth, New Jersey 07206 ▪ 908.965.3108

June 12, 2005

It's very thoughtful to let the reference know how the job search turned out.

Madhu N. Mehta, Pharm.D.
Assistant Professor of Pharmacy
Rutgers, the State University of New Jersey
College of Pharmacy
242 Frelinguysen Road
Piscataway, New Jersey 08855-0634

Dear Dr. Mehta:

I am pleased to inform you that I accepted an offer of employment with HLM Managed Care, Inc. in Cherry Hill as a clinical account manager. I begin my new position on August 1, 2005.

I appreciate all of your assistance during the past several months in serving as a reference and helping me evaluate the merits of different offers.

Again, thank you for all you have done to advance my career.

Sincerely,

Courtney K. Moore, Pharm.D.

Actual letter size is 8.5 x 11

A letter following up on an interview, which serves as a cover letter for a portfolio CD-ROM.
Font: Univers 14 point.

Mark A. Williamson
2581 Courtland Terrace, Kokomo, IN 47802
(765) 868-6504   mawilli3@purdue.edu

January 25, 2005

Ruth G. Harrison, M.S.
Director of Pharmacy Services
Montgomery Regional Hospital
2105 Rosewood Boulevard
Montgomery, AL 36116

Calling the recipient's attention to the letter's subject can be useful when you are following up on a previous meeting or interaction.

Re: Resident Match Number 13579

Dear Ms. Harrison:

Thank you for inviting me to interview for your pharmacy practice residency program. I appreciate the time that you and your staff devoted to me during the day-long interview session.

I am very interested in completing a pharmacy practice residency under your guidance. I have enclosed a CD-ROM containing my portfolio, which provides additional information about my educational accomplishments and professional practice development during the past six years.

Please let me know if your staff needs additional information from me before you conclude the residency match process.

Sincerely,

Mark A. Williamson

Appendix

Supplementary Information Sources

A wealth of reference materials exist about career planning, interviewing skills, and preparing correspondence. Although most of these publications have been prepared with the business community in mind, the principles apply to other professionals, as well. The sources in the following reference list may provide useful information.

Career Planning

APhA Career Pathway Evaluation Program for Pharmacy Professionals. 5th ed. Washington: American Pharmacists Association; 2005.

Baker WE. Networking Smart. Lincoln, Nebraska: Backinprint.com; 2000.

Bolles RN. What Color is Your Parachute? A Practical Manual for Job-Hunters and Career-Changers. 35th ed. Berkeley: Ten Speed Press; 2005.

Bolles RN. Job Hunting on the Internet. 4th ed. Berkeley: Ten Speed Press; 2005.

Double DL. Assessing Your Career Options. Chicago: American Medical Association; 1998.

Ellis D. Creating Your Future: Five Steps to the Life of Your Dreams. New York: Houghton Mifflin Co; 1999.

Fox MR, Morton P. Job Search 101. Indianapolis: JIST Works, Inc; 1997.

Gurney DW. Headhunters Revealed! Los Angeles: Hunter Arts Publishing; 2000.

Heiberger MM, Vick JM. The Academic Job Search Handbook. 3rd ed. Philadelphia: University of Pennsylvania Press; 2001.

Knowdell RL. Building a Career Development Program. Palo Alto: Davies-Black Publishing; 1996.

Krannich CR, Krannich RL. Dynamite Networking for Dynamite Jobs. Manassas Park, Virginia: Impact Publications; 1996.

Moses B. Career Intelligence. San Francisco: Berrett-Koehler Publishers, Inc; 1998.

Schommer JC, Brown LM, Millonig MK, Sogol EM. Career Pathways Evaluation Program: 2002 Pharmacist Profile Survey, Am J Pharm Ed. 2003; 67: Article 79.

Sowers-Hoag K, Harrison DF. Finding an Academic Job. Thousand Oaks, California: SAGE Publications, Inc; 1998.

Tulliver LM. Networking for Everyone Job Search and Career Services. 2nd ed. Indianapolis: JIST Works, Inc; 2004.

Preparing Résumés and Curricula Vitae

Asher D. The Overnight Résumé. 2nd ed. Berkeley: Ten Speed Press; 1999.

Asher D. Asher's Bible of Executive Résumés and How to Write Them. Berkeley: Ten Speed Press; 1997.

Bernard Haldane Associates. Haldane's Best Résumés for Professionals. Manassas Park, Virginia: Impact Publications; 1999.

Block JA, Betrus M. 202 Great Résumés. Washington, D.C.: McGraw-Hill Companies, Inc; 2004.

Block JA, Betrus M. 101 Best Résumés to Sell Yourself. Washington, D.C.: McGraw-Hill Companies, Inc; 2002.

Corwin G, Grappo GJ, Lewis A. How to Write Better Résumés. 6th ed. New York: McGraw-Hill Companies, Inc.; 2003.

Criscito P. Résumés in Cyberspace. 2nd ed. Hauppauge, New York: Barron's Educational Series, Inc.; 2000.

Criscito P. e-Résumés: A Guide to Successful Online Job Hunting. 3rd ed. Hauppauge, New York: Barron's Educational Series, Inc.; 2004.

Criscito P. *Designing the Perfect Résumé*. 3rd ed. Hauppauge, New York: Barron's Educational Series, Inc.; 2005.

Enelow WS, Kursmark LM. *Expert Résumés for People Returning to Work*. Indianapolis: JIST Works, Inc.; 2003.

Enelow WS, Kursmark LM. *Expert Résumés for Career Changers*. Indianapolis: JIST Works, Inc.; 2005.

Enelow WS. *Résumé Winners from the Pros*. Manassas Park, Virginia: Impact Publications; 1998.

Enelow WS. *Best Key Words for Résumés, Cover Letters and Interviews: Powerful Communications Tools for Success*. Manassas Park, Virginia: Impact Publications; 2003.

Farr JM. *America's Top Résumés for America's Top Jobs*. 2nd ed. Indianapolis: JIST Works, Inc; 2002.

Farr JM. *The Quick Résumé and Cover Letter Book*. 2nd ed. Indianapolis: JIST Works, Inc; 2000.

Grappo GJ, Lewis A. *How to Write Better Résumés*. 5th ed. Hauppauge, New York: Barron's Educational Series, Inc; 1998.

Greene B. *Get the Interview Every Time*. Chicago: Dearborn Trade Publishing; 2004.

Hamilton L. *Wow Résumés for Health Careers*. Washington, D.C.: McGraw-Hill Companies, Inc; 1998.

Ireland S. *The Complete Idiot's Guide to the Perfect Résumé*. 3rd ed. New York: Penguin Putnam, Inc; 2003.

Isaacs K, Hofferber K. *The Career Change Résumé*. New York: McGraw-Hill Companies, Inc.; 2003.

Jackson AL. *How to Prepare Your Curriculum Vitae*. Chicago: NTC Learning Works; 2003.

Jackson AL, Geckeis K. *How to Prepare Your Curriculum Vitae*. 3rd ed. New York: McGraw-Hill Companies, Inc.; 2003.

Jackson T, Jackson E. *The New Perfect Résumé*. New York: Doubleday; 1996.

Kaplan RM. *Résumé Shortcuts*. Manassas Park, Virginia: Impact Publications; 1997.

Kennedy JL. *Résumés for Dummies*. 4th ed. Foster City, California: IDG Books Worldwide, Inc; 2002.

Krannich RL, Enelow WS. *Best Résumés and CVs for International Jobs*. Manassas Park, Virginia: Impact Publications; 2002.

Krannich RL, Banis WJ. *High Impact Résumés and Letters*. 9th ed. Manassas Park, Virginia: Impact Publications; 2005.

Marino K. *Résumés for the Health Care Professional*. New York: John Wiley and Sons, Inc; 2000.

Nadler BJ. *The Everything Résumé Book*. 2nd ed. Avon, Massachusetts: Adams Media; 2003.

Noble DF. *Professional Résumés for Executives, Managers, and Other Administrators*. Indianapolis: JIST Works, Inc; 1998.

Noble DF. *Gallery of Best Résumés*. 3rd ed. Indianapolis: JIST Works Inc; 2004.

Parker Y. *The Résumé Catalog: 200 Damn Good Examples*. Berkeley: Ten Speed Press; 1998.

Provenzano SA. *Top Secret Executive Résumés*. Franklin Lakes, New Jersey: The Career Press, Inc; 2000.

Ryan R. *Winning Résumés*. 2nd ed. New York: John Wiley and Sons, Inc; 2002.

Smith MH. *The Résumé Writer's Handbook*. 2nd ed. New York: HarperCollins Publishers; 1987.

Tepper R. *Power Résumés*. 3rd ed. New York: John Wiley and Sons, Inc; 1998.

Troutman KK. *The Federal Résumé Guidebook: Write a Winning Federal Résumé to Get in, Get Promoted, and Survive in a Government Career!* Indianapolis: JIST Works, Inc; 2004.

Troutman KK. *Electronic Federal Résumé Guidebook*. Indianapolis: JIST Works, Inc; 2001.

Tysinger JW. *Résumés and Personal Statements for Health Professionals*. 2nd ed. Tucson: Galen Press, Ltd; 1999.

VGM Career Horizons. *Résumés for Health and Medical Careers*. 2nd ed. Washington, D.C.: McGraw Hill; 1999.

VGM Career Horizons. *Résumés for Scientific and Technical Careers*. 2nd ed. Washington, D.C.: McGraw Hill; 2001.

Wendleton K. *Building a Great Résumé*. 2nd ed. New York: The Five O'Clock Club, Inc; 1999.

Whitcomb SB. *Résumé Magic: Trade Secrets of a Professional Résumé Writer.* Indianapolis: JIST Works, Inc; 2003.

Wilson RF, Lewis A. *Better Résumés for Executives and Professionals.* 4th ed. Hauppauge, New York: Barron's Educational Series, Inc; 2000.

Yenney SL. *The Physician's Résumé and Cover Letter Workbook.* Chicago: American Medical Association; 1998.

Interviewing Skills

Allen JG. *The Complete Q & A Job Interview Book.* 3rd ed. New York: John Wiley and Sons, Inc; 2000.

Ball FW, Ball BB. *Killer Interviews.* Washington, D.C.: McGraw-Hill Companies, Inc; 1996.

Beatty RH. *The Interview Kit.* 3rd ed. New York: John Wiley and Sons, Inc; 2003.

Beatty RH. *Interviewing and Selecting High Performers: Every Manager's Guide to Effective Interviewing Techniques.* New York: John Wiley and Sons, Inc; 1994.

Camp R, Vielhaber ME, Simonetti JL. *Strategic Interviewing.* San Francisco: Jossey-Bass, Inc.; 2001.

Corcodilos NA. *Ask the Headhunter—Reinventing the Interview to Win the Job.* New York: Penguin Putnam, Inc; 1997.

DeLuca MJ. *Best Answers to the 201 Most Frequently Asked Interview Questions.* Washington, D.C.: McGraw-Hill Companies, Inc; 2001.

Drake J. *The Perfect Interview: How to Get the Job You Really Want.* 2nd ed. New York: AMACOM; 1997.

Eyler DR. *Job Interviews That Mean Business.* 3rd ed. New York: Random House, Inc; 1999.

Fein R. *101 Dynamite Questions to Ask at Your Job Interview.* 2nd ed. Manassas Park, Virginia: Impact Publications; 2000.

Fry R. *101 Great Answers to the Toughest Interview Questions.* 4th ed. Franklin Lakes, New Jersey: The Carter Press, Inc; 2000.

Gottesman D, Mauro B. *The Interview Rehearsal Book.* New York: The Berkley Publishing Group; 1999.

Hirsch A. *Interviewing—Effective Techniques to Help You Answer Tough Questions and Make a Great Impression.* New York: John Wiley and Sons, Inc; 1994.

Kador J. *201 Best Questions to Ask on Your Interview.* New York: McGraw-Hill Companies, Inc.; 2002.

Kanter AB. *The Essential Book of Interviewing.* New York: Random House, Inc; 1995.

Kennedy JL. *Job Interviews for Dummies.* 2nd ed. New York: IDG Books Worldwide, Inc.; 2000.

Krannich CR, Krannich RL. *Interview for Success.* 8th ed. Manassas Park, Virginia: Impact Publications; 2002.

Krannich CR, Krannich RL. *101 Dynamite Answers to Interview Questions.* Manassas Park, Virginia: Impact Publications; 1999.

McKay DR. *The Everything Practice Interview Book.* Avon, Massachusetts: Adams Media; 2004.

Martin C. *Boost Your Interview IQ.* New York: McGraw-Hill; 2004.

Medley HA. *Sweaty Palms—The Neglected Art of Being Interviewed.* New York: Warner Business Books; 2005.

Veruki P. *The 250 Job Interview Questions You'll Most Likely Be Asked and the Answers That Will Get You Hired!* Holbrook, Massachusetts: Adams Media Corporation; 1999.

Wilson RF. *Conducting Better Job Interviews.* 2nd ed. Hauppauge, New York: Barron's Educational Series, Inc; 1997.

Yates M. *Knock 'em Dead 2005: The Ultimate Job Seekers Guide.* Holbrook, Massachusetts: Adams Media Corporation; 2005.

Yeager N, Hough L. *Power Interviews.* New York: John Wiley and Sons, Inc; 1998.

Preparing Correspondence

Beatty RH. *The Perfect Cover Letter.* 3rd ed. New York: John Wiley and Sons, Inc; 2003.

Beatty RH. *175 High-Impact Cover Letters.* 3rd ed. New York: John Wiley and Sons, Inc; 2002.

Block JA, Betrus M. *101 Best Cover Letters*. Washington, D.C.: McGraw-Hill Companies, Inc; 1999.

Bly RW. *The Encyclopedia of Business Letters, Fax Memos, and E-Mail*. Franklin Lakes, New Jersey: Career Press; 1999.

Enelow WS. *201 Winning Cover Letters for $100,000+ Jobs*. Manassas Park, Virginia: Impact Publications; 1998.

Heller B. *The 100 Most Difficult Business Letters You'll Ever Have to Write, Fax, or E-Mail*. New York: HarperCollins Publishers, Inc; 1994.

Ireland S. *The Complete Idiot's Guide to the Perfect Cover Letter*. New York: Simon and Schuster Macmillan Co; 1997.

Kennedy JL. *Cover Letters for Dummies*. 2nd ed. New York: Hungry Minds, Inc.; 2000.

Noble DF. *Gallery of Best Cover Letters*. 3rd ed. Indianapolis: JIST Works, Inc; 2004.

Podesta S, Paxton A. *201 Killer Cover Letters*. 2nd ed. Washington, D.C.: McGraw-Hill Companies, Inc; 2003.

Wynett S. *Cover Letters That Will Get You the Job You Want*. Cincinnati: Better Way Books; 1993.

Yates M. *Cover Letters That Knock 'em Dead*. 6th ed. Holbrook, Massachusetts: Adams Media Corporation; 2004.

Preparing Career Statements

Richardson J. *Mastering the Personal Statement*. Toronto: Richardson Press; 2000.

Stelzer RJ. *How to Write a Winning Personal Statement for Graduate and Professional School*. 3rd ed. Lawrenceville, New Jersey: Thomson Peterson's; 1997.

Stewart MA. *Perfect Personal Statements*. 3rd ed. Lawrenceville, New Jersey: Thomson Peterson's; 2004.

Preparing Portfolios

Campbell DM, Cignetti PB, Melenyzer BJ, Nettles DH, Wyman RM. *How to Develop a Professional Portfolio*. 3rd ed. New York: Pearson Education, Inc.; 2004.

Costantino PM, DeLorenzo MN. *Developing a Professional Teaching Portfolio—A Guide to Success*. Boston: Allyn and Bacon; 2005.

Seldin P. *The Teaching Portfolio—A Practical Guide to Improved Performance and Promotion/Tenure Decisions*. 3rd ed. Boston: Anker Publishing Company, Inc.; 2004.

Professional Image

Caspersson DM. *Power Etiquette—What You Don't Know Can Kill Your Career*. Washington: American Management Association International; 1999.

Hammer DP, Berger BA, Beardsley RS, Easton MR: Student Professionalism. *Am J Pharm Educ*. 2003: 67 (3) Article 96.

Post P. *Essential Manners for Men*. New York: Harper-Collins Publishers, Inc.; 2003.

Ramsey L. *Manners That Sell—Adding the Polish That Builds Profits*. Savannah: Longfellow Press; 2003.

Seitz VA. *Your Executive Image*. 2nd ed. Holbrook, Massachusetts: Adams Media Corporation; 2000.

Thourlby W. *You Are What You Wear*. New York: Forbes/Wittenburg and Brown; 1995.

General Reference

Baker K, Baker S. *How to Say It Online*. Paramus, New Jersey: Prentice Hall Press; 2001.

Lindsell-Roberts S, Stevens MA. *Merriam Webster's Secretarial Handbook*. 3rd ed. Springfield, Massachusetts: Merriam-Webster, Inc; 1993.

Publication Manual of the American Psychological Association. 5th ed. Washington: American Psychological Association; 2001.

Sabin WA. *The Gregg Reference Manual*. 10th ed. New York: The McGraw-Hill Companies; 2005.

Strunk W, White EB. *The Elements of Style*. 4th ed. Needham Heights, Massachusetts: Allyn and Bacon; 2000.

Style Manual. 29th ed. Washington, D.C.: United States Government Printing Office; 2000.

The Chicago Manual of Style. 15th ed. Chicago: The University of Chicago Press; 2003.

Index